Henry Buss

Wanderings in the West

during the year 1870

Henry Buss

Wanderings in the West
during the year 1870

ISBN/EAN: 9783744650861

Printed in Europe, USA, Canada, Australia, Japan

Cover: Foto ©Andreas Hilbeck / pixelio.de

More available books at **www.hansebooks.com**

WANDERINGS

IN THE

WEST,

DURING THE YEAR 1870.

BY

H. BUSS, M.D.,

ETC., ETC.

Printed for Private Circulation by

THOMAS DANKS, 9, CRANE COURT,

FLEET STREET, LONDON.

1871.

SUBJECTS.

—•◦▶◀◦•—

THE AUTHOR TO HIS FRIENDS.

AFFLICTION dipped in sable ink her pen ;
Stern sentence 'gainst the Author then was written ;
So must it be with all the sons of men,
When kindred dear by ruthless Death are smitten.

Travel, now kindly tendering him her aid
By rapid change through distant scene and clime,
New thoughts begat, sad memories caused to fade :
Wise resignation slowly came with time.
Still, often would unwelcome Solitude
Unveil the past before sad Memory's eye ;
And Sorrow, uninvited, would intrude,
Gaze on the scene and raise the heart-felt sigh !

Then came an Influence, sometimes felt before—
A stirring spirit-whispering in the ear,

"Thou shalt not be alone for evermore—
Invoke thy Muse, thee company to bear."

When Muse bears company by man's desire
To chase away both solitude and grief,
'Tis rare she breathes with high poetic fire—
'Tis not essential for the sought relief.
Thus with the Author.—This relief obtained,
Unto the flames the manuscript was due:
But friends, whom partiality had gained,
Begged of his "Wanderings" copies—just a few.
So them to please, but not the critic's eye,
The manuscript was typed, in cloth was dressed.
The Author hopes there's no immodesty
In offering these, his "Wanderings in the West."

WANDERINGS

IN THE WEST.

EXODUS.

I.

The fiery steed of the North-Western train
Bears us away from Modern Babylon,
  'Neath street, and square, and over many a lane,
At forty miles an hour: and, then, upon
  The country plains as far as Willesden.
A mighty junction this, above, below;
  Baffling poor dames and simple countrymen.
These hesitating, hurry to and fro;
The engine screams aloud, and off the monsters go!

II.

At such great speed, 'tis soon at Rugby Junction.
But as the speed is, so the oscillation;
　Each holds his seat and dreads its altered function.
Passed is Nuneaton, so is Stafford station.
　The gastric wants must be attended to;
Some swallow coffee hot, some ices cool:
　The bounding train pulls up for this at Crewe;
Then plunges on again, since speed does rule.
Five hours such as this you're safe in Liverpool.

III.

Give Chanticleer good time to call his mates,
Ere you arise, and take your morning bath.
　Arrange for shipboard,—satisfy its rates;
Should time permit, townwards direct your path.
　There's much in Liverpool to claim attention,—
St. George's Hall; Docks, which enormous grow;
　The 'Change stupendous, and of high invention;
The pontoon-landings, which float high or low,
Just as the Mersey's tide doth daily ebb or flow.

IV.

The time approaches for your ship to sail;
Its tender, urged by steam, draws alongside;
   Anxiety just whispers, "Don't you fail
To be on board in time: you have to ride
   Three thousand miles in yonder gallant bark."
Trunks, packages, and baskets in *galore;*
   Companions, of all nations, fair and dark,
Are crowding on the quay; then, more and more
In vehicles, on foot, are pressing to the shore.

V.

The tender off, is now the ship beside,—
A huge leviathan,—she stands so high!
   The British flag astern floats in just pride;
Her spire-masts soar up towards the sky;
   The pennants at the gallant-tops seem strings;
The crew and passengers the decks now throng:
   Her tender quits,—again, again it brings
More and more freight, for each time is not long—
So fast its paddles turn, cheered by the steam-throat song.

VI.

The Mersey here is wide ; its tidal flood
Gives occupation to a fleet of boats ;　　　　　[stood,
　　Large wharves and docks abound where marsh once
And in these docks commercial giants float.
　　This view is charming from the upper deck,—
The river is astir with ferry craft,
　　And parting friends stretch eyes, and head, and neck,
Scanning the steamer o'er from fore to aft; [laughed.
Most shed some fare well tears,—but few there were who

VII.

Two thousand years ago, when Æsop old
Wrote of the waggoner who was not able
　　To extricate the wheels, he only told
A world-wide truth, albeit 'twas a fable.
　　The heathen godhead,—naughty, goat-like Jove,—
Ordered the clown "not like a child to squeal,
　　But having strength and will, it him behove
To put his sturdy shoulders to the wheel."
The teaching of this moral all the world can feel.

VIII.

This moral well was felt some century back,
When the wise genius of Liverpool
Saw that its men nor will nor force did lack,
Suggested to their minds the golden rule,—
"God will help all who will themselves to aid."
The inspir'd council then replanned the town;
Large moles projected. Thus, the Mersey made
To form two miles of docks, which since have grown;
Commerce approved the act, and hence its great renown.

IX.

All cargo is on board, the steam is up,—
Still clings the tender to the side of ship.
The first bell rings; some take the parting cup;
Many a tear, a hug, a farewell grip!
Th' impatient engine shrieks out more and more,
And ling'ring friends still grasp each other's hand.
The call repeated, "Any more for shore"?
And loiterer last doth on the tender stand.
The second bell hath rung,—the tender seeks the land.

x.

What anxious, loving glances interchange
'Twixt couples joined in wedlock's holy bond,

As distance draws them out of vision's range;—
'Twixt sever'd kindred too, and friendships fond!

Love, Interest, Duty, Fear, Ambition, Hate,
Provoke the Fates to will each exodus.

What strong emotions on their owners wait,
For future trials, and for parting thus!—
Their shipboard joys and sorrows let us now discuss.

THE "DENMARK."

I.

THE steamer "Denmark" is a ship of might;
Close on four hundred feet she boasts of length;
Four storeys full, she rears herself in height;
While forty feet of beam insures her strength.
Her steeple masts soar up towards the sky.
Urged by a power of four hundred horse,
With fifty tons of coal they daily ply
Her Vulcan throats to stimulate her course:
And well her giant limbs transmit such Titan force.

II.

But see the world within! a town indeed!
A thousand souls—Celt, from the Emerald soil,
    The fair-haired Saxon, Belgian, Dane, and Swede,
Off to the distant west, by honest toil
    Their fortunes to improve.   The varied crew
Is officered right well; each duty done
    Exact as clockwork—efficiency, the due
Of rigid discipline.   So, the Atlantic run
In the good ship "Denmark" is thus a hopeful one.

III.

Look down the hatchway, how the steps they seize!
Just at the hour when 'tis feeding time,
    What motley streams of life; like children-bees
Threading the hives, as shown in pantomime.
    Endless it seems, until it meets a check;
Each with his glittering can for soupy ration,
    Down from the upper to the orlop deck,
Wending his way into his proper station,
Like worthy citizens of a well-ordered nation.

IV.

At first all seems confused; but, by and bye,
Each trunk and box and bag is stowed away;
  The all-devouring hold is made to try
Its swallowing capacity. Ere close of day,
  Two thousand tons of coal and other freight
Are quietly disposed : all in their place,
  The emigrants as well, with all their weight;
Sadness or hope, depicted in each face,
As thoughts of past or future leave behind their trace.

V.

At length, the anchor weighed, the "Denmark" sails,
Down from the Mersey, through the Irish Sea;
  On the port-side hugging the coast of Wales,
With numerous sea-gulls keeping company.
  The following day the Emerald Isle we view;
Ere Phœbus set, Queenstown is on our lee;
  Letters dispatched, the pilot bold and true
Quits in his gig; the last of land we see—
Nought but the endless main, type of Eternity!

VI.

The following morn, the gulls, reduced to eight,
Follow the vessel's wake.   But their eccentric flight,
  Makes fifty miles an hour—so far from straight !
On gaily bounds the bark, so trim so tight;
  At half five hundred miles from nearest shore
The last and strongest gull quacks his farewell.
  The surging billows roll the steamer o'er ;
And many heaving stomachs sink and swell;
Doing so many things their owners blush to tell.

VII.

'Tis not recorded, whether, when the gods
Exchanged their visits in celestial spheres
  Toll-tax existed.   Probably, the odds
Are much against that notion.   Still, for years
  Frail mortals have been mulcted of such toll.
Charon required pay when, o'er the Styx,
  He pulled to Hades each departed soul.
Now, 'neath the sea somewhere, Neptune doth fix,
His palace all of pearl ; it can't be made of bricks.

VIII.

'Tis not quite clear whether by Jove's permit,
But certain 'tis, that such as cross the main,
   Are mostly summoned, if Neptune should see fit,
To pay the tribute to his mighty reign.
   'Tis very odd how much mankind dislikes
To pay a tribute, tax, or any toll
   On property, or income, sewers, turnpikes,
Water or gas; game, customs, or *a poll.*
At sea, 'tis just the same, none likes to give his dole.

IX.

Neptune is monarch,—a right royal swell!
Used to command; expects to be obeyed:
   He tribute wants; collectors con it well;
All gusty spirits these that know their trade.
   Full dash they bounce against the starboard stern;
The captain sees the move; up go the sails,
   At Boatswain's whistle; round the wheel doth turn;
The ship cants to the wind, and so, the rails   [vails.
Are clutched by many wights, who seek to shirk its

x.

Some men are obstinate, and much object
To give to Neptune what is Neptune's due;
   They press their mouths, and don't a bit reflect,
How gastric servants, steady, firm and true,
   Dislike retaining what they can't digest:
These claim from Diaphragm a speedy aid;
   Convince it also, that for them 'tis best,
To square accounts. So, thus the toll is paid:—
A gripe, twitch, spasm,—the stomach is easy made.

xi.

In the Atlantic when the sky is clear,
The sea is blue; but not so deep a blue,
   As doth the Mediterranean appear:
Whose very deep blue sky,—the azure true,
   Reflects its tint upon the placid main.
When clouded, it is leaden. You may see,
   The sand or rock, whichever one doth gain,
Tinting the waters,—as the case may be,—
Green, yellow, brown or white, in great variety.

XII.

When austral zephyrs fill the sails with wind,
And clouds are not, but Phœbus smiles his best,
  The ailing passengers on deck you'll find,
Like acrobats, essaying with a zest
  Their balance to maintain.   If boreal blasts
Sweep o'er the decks, that which is fun to them
  Makes mortals shiver.   While their fury lasts
Great coats are buttoned with a manifest phlegm.
Pale faces leeward stream, e'en Phœbus can't this stem.

XIII.

When the just tribute which old Neptune claims,
Has been collected in the foaming deep,
  And sturdy gentlemen and gentler dames
Can laugh and joke, and eat and drink and sleep;
  They lack amusement.   Some *ship-billiards* try,
For table—deck, on which they numbers score,
  For balls—flat discs of wood, which quickly fly,
Urged by long mallets o'er the polished floor.
This game so popular, is now played more and more.

XIV.

Another game on board, one to amuse,
Is quoits—ship quoits, in which some few are skilled.
    The quoits are rings of rope, well kept for use ;
Not the steel ring which ancient worthy killed.
    A wooden board, on which is fixed a peg,
Is placed on deck : the player takes in hand
    The hempen rings, and poising well on leg,
Pitches each quoit on to the peggy stand :
And those who peg the most obtain the chief command.

XV.

Sometimes at night, there's acting, dance, charades ;
A curtain fixed to form a mimic stage ;
    With recitations from the choicest bards ;
And songs—the offspring of the lyric page.
    Music as well is oft extemporized—
Failing piano, which often you will find.
    Puzzling conundrums are at all times prized ;
And riddles droll, of every varied kind ;   [mind.
With stories told 'bout ghosts, to soothe the youthful

XVI.

The Western Boreas now withdraws his blow,
And austral zephyrs soon inflate their cheeks;
  The sturdy engines still more mighty grow,
Doing in days what once required weeks.
  The sullen clouds disperse; the orb of day
Shines with refulgence, as in days of yore;
  The convalescents quit their berths, and say
They ne'er enjoyed themselves so much before.
So gallantly the waves this worthy ship skims o'er.

XVII.

It ofttimes happened that Aurora, veil'd,
Too long continued coy; the god of day
  Beamed forth his sunny smiles, which rarely failed
To make the coquette draw the veil away.
  And sometimes too, when Phœbus sank to rest,
The winds would on the deck their vigils keep,
  Straining the foremast sheets towards the west;
The graceful prow would curtsey in the deep,
Rocking poor convalescents into troubled sleep.

XVIII.

Ambrosia is food for gods ! nectar they quaff;
Sometimes, while feasting at Olympian revels,
   Immortals chaste would take too much by half,
And then their god-like acts were those of devils.
   One night this naughty conduct tossed our ship;
Gluttonous Neptune exceeded his right share,
   His ocean bed so up and down did dip;
Sure he was drunk, unless he had the nightmare;
For mortal stomachs weak this was not the right fare.

XIX.

'Twas not a god-like act, 'twas not done well,
To roll the " Denmark " o'er from side to side ;
   " O never mind, Ma'am, 'tis but Neptune's swell,"
The steward to timid matron straight replied.
   I almost from my berth fell out with laughter,
As bags each other chevied round the floor ;
   Some of the berths their burthens shot out after,
Unceremoniously against the door !   [sore.
The " Denmark's " timbers groaned and grunted very

XX.

Westward the " Denmark " steams as day by day
She glides along upon the bubbling foam,
And gallantly doth dash aside the spray,
Raising her ensign to all ships passing home.
As coachmen recognise the passers by,
And courteous gentlemen their hats will raise ;
So Neptune's sons with other courtiers vie,
Bending the knee to fashion, as is the case
At court, upon the bench, in camp, and holy place.

XXI.

And when our orb twice seven times had turned,
" Fire Island lighthouse " bringing into view ;
When anxious hearts for shore so long have burned ;
The navigators all so staunch and true ;
We reach the long-wished port, our luggage clear,
And quit our friends with silent, heartfelt grip ;
Grateful to God for His protecting care ;
Thanking the officers and crew of ship.   [trip.
" God speed to all !" we say—then onward with our

NEW ORLEANS.

I.

BRIGHT New Orleans!
Well placed on Mississippi's bank ;
Less fair than France, thou still dost rank
One of Columbia's queens !
Here, Commerce caused thy river's flank
To be well clothed with miles of plank—
Finding both mind and means.

II.

Majestic flood !
By thee the first adventurous band,
Which sought this Mississippi land,
    Of Gallia's race and blood,
Upon the marge of thy left hand,
Was helped to plant a city grand,
    From France's parent bud.

III.

As Time toiled on,
Adventure, flying o'er the west,
Gazed down, resolved to put a test
    Its citizens upon :
She incense shook—this gave a zest
To cotton growth, which drew in quest
    The sons of Albion.

IV.

Her townsmen took
Straightway the hint Adventure gave,
With capital and Afric's slave
    Seed of tobacco shook:
So raised a weed the world doth crave,
And sent it o'er Atlantic wave,
      To every smoker's nook.

V.

    Success could see,
How all the vast luxuriant ground,
For many hundred miles around,
    Pregnant with wealth might be.
The river's sides were kept in bound,
Millions of bales fit stowage found,
    On its enormous quay.

VI.

These cotton bales,
Mass'd in a heap on the broad quay;
Brought there by river, rail, and sea,
For periodic sales.
Each heap known by a flag must be,
Of owner's name, or argosy,
Waiting propitious gales.

VII.

Where else beside,
Such gangs of dusky labour free,
Compelled by stern necessity
Their sloth to override?
In this warm clime, where Liberty
Shakes negro's hands fraternally,
Men feel, not follow pride!

VIII.

Here, Commerce brings
From all the mighty watershed,
By which the Mississippi's fed,
    All sorts of valued things.
Ships, cars and boats, by steam are led
To carry hence,—and bring instead,
    Of trade—all offerings!

IX.

Time puts his seal
Upon the ancient quarter—French,
Where, streets and shops and market-bench
    Are Gallicis'd, we feel.
Change to the West has failed to wrench
The Gallic pluck, or e'en to quench,
    Their love of the Ideal!

X.

Here, too, belongs
The negro quarter, off whose hands
Freedom has struck the iron bands,
    And many other wrongs. .
And now, the negro understands,
That freedom too, obeys commands,
    And joins in labour's throngs.

XI.

The Irish, too,
In numbers great, are gathered here;
And in their quarter, as elsewhere,
    Act as they always do :
When strikes have made their market dear,
And rival toil is, brought—they swear,
    Such liberty is not true.

XII.

Since late sad war,
North-Eastern men of enterprise,
Seek New-Orleans to make uprise,—
    Yet, still more prosp'rous far.
Skill, energy—the Yankee tries ;
'Cute, firm and prompt—his zeal applies,
    For seat in Fortune's car.

XIII.

All the new part
Is well displayed,—wide road and street,
Where Yankee-families now meet,
    With modest taste and art.
French dialects your ear will greet,
In all old quarters, still the seat
    Of Gallia's children smart.

XIV.

The town being low,
In all wide streets, the iron-way
For cars with single mule, they lay;
 Nor is their travel slow:
Important is the part they play,
By running for so small a pay,
 To where the suburbs grow.

———•———

COLUMBIA.

I.

COLUMBIA ! I have landed on thy shore,
Partaken of thy hospitality,
    Seen thy huge cataracts and heard them roar ;
Steam'd up thy rivers teeming with vitality ;
    View'd thy large harbours, where, in all their pride,
Safely secured from outward ocean storm,
    The mightiest ships of all the world can ride,
Or quit their freight in docks of varied form,
Which, from the shore projected, now so densely swarm.

II.

Where else than in thy waters can be seen,
Hotels five storeys high—as ships afloat,
  Whose drawing rooms, three hundred feet have been
Arranged in length? To realise a boat
  'Midst elegant saloons is difficult;
With mirror'd-panels set in gilded moulds,
  Satin and rosewoods chisell'd,—the result
Of taste luxurious. Much in white and gold,
With ottomans and carpets at a cost untold!

III.

'Midst elegance like this, Columbia sees
Her citizens downwards to the humblest wight
  Enjoying their Republic at their ease;
Freedom and equality for their birthright.
  And if, sometimes, licentiousness is able
To coax free men their quid of juice to share,
  Or loll their lanky legs upon the table;
Columbia breathes a sigh, lets fall a tear,
Well knowing for the future, there is nought to fear.

IV.

Few harbours are more active than New York's,
Studded with boats, high mounted up in ridges,
   Like graceful swans, they float as light as corks,
Joining the shores opposed the same as bridges.
   Vehicles of every shape, and size, and kind,
In any number are conveyed thereby;
   Human and every other freight, you'll find
Going and coming to the ferries nigh;
And this too, very oft, so great their industry.

.V.

   Here, pigmy steamers (yachts of private men),
Will for salutes, give out three slender squeaks
   To giant steamboats passing.   These will then
Return three roars so loud—each vessel shrieks,
   As on it plunges to its destination
With its enormous load of man and beast,
   And produce brought from each surrounding station,
From Europe, Afric, and the distant east;
To adorn the body, and the body feast.

VI.

A tiny tug, urged by the giant steam,
To monster with three masts, too large for fear,
  Will saucily make up, then 'thwart a beam
Fling arm of hemp.   And now, like Chanticleer,
  Will puff and spit, and crow, a cock-a-doodle ;
Carrying off Brobdingnag who just looks down,
  From his high eminence,—dejected noodle !
Half scornfully, yet with Hyperion frown
On the proud Lilliput, at once so bumptious grown.

VII.

Columbia ! thy metropolis, New York,
With European towns doth well compare ;
  Grand is thy Broadway-street, wherein do walk,
The New York belles, whose beauty is most rare,
  Their profiles finely chiselled.   Intellect
With firmness joining in high brow, and chin [effect,
  Rounded and prominent.   They dress with great
Handsome decidedly,—a " wee " bit thin,—
A question this of taste, most men will differ in.

VIII.

The houses are built in blocks, at angles right,
Which margined are by streets and avenues,—
   Avenues so long as to evade the sight;
And named by numbers,—each situation true
   Thereby is indicated. Then, the streets
Begin with *first*, and mount to any height;
   Thus without trouble every stranger meets
The avenue, the street, the house all right:
A system for precision this that answers quite.

IX.

In all new states, where Ceres is besought
To yield to Agriculture golden sheaves,
   Necessities of life with comforts fraught
Are all she grants at first. She later leaves
   Embellishment of country, hill, and dale,
Till Time has leisure to attend her call;
   Then smiling Flora yields her glittering trail,
Adorning homesteads, beautifying all,—
Whilst Sculpture lends her art the senses to enthral.

x.

So in the eastern and some northern States
Has Time, though old, untired, toiled along;
　Each of the Graces on this monarch waits;
Thus are his footprints followed by a throng
　That homage yield to Genius, Fashion, Pride;
And so the eye is charmed, when by the rail
　You pass through cities for a country ride.
Luxurious tastes have been of great avail—
Villas and parks are met, with lakes and many a sail.

xi.

Wide are the streets in Philadelphia,
But much less so in busy Baltimore.
　Whenever rivers, or the sea comes near,
There wharves and docks uprise along the shore.
　Many and large, their markets have upgrown
For vending produce of Columbia's land.
　Parks, squares, fine statues, both in bronze and stone,
Imposing churches and cathedrals grand,
Whence holy strains ascend from many a choral band.

XII.

Columbia's capital is Washington.
On a high site its Capitol is reared;
   Simple in style, but of conception grand,
It to her patriots has become endeared.
   Vast in its length, its dome soars to the skies,
And brilliant with illumination shines;
   Noble, majestic, with our St. Paul's it vies;
The marble front with iron dome combines;
Projecting porticos diversify its lines.

XIII.

Few capitols can boast so high a site!
For miles around this glorious pile is seen
   Crowning the city in its pride and might.
Of capitols, it is Columbia's Queen!
   Its corridor prolonged from end to end,
Full seven hundred feet, is very wide.
   The central hall doth 'neath the dome extend,
Embellished with war trophies, side by side
Of limners' and sculptors' art, justly Columbia's pride.

XIV.

The Senate-House forms one end of the pile;
The Congress hall is at the end opposed,
  State offices are simple in their style,
Its ample galleries to none are closed,
  Free is admission, no one needs to wait;
The Press is well accommodated too.
  Debates in both departments of the state
Women may freely hear—without caged pew,—
Or members' order—or vails to official crew.

XV.

So with the docks and all their public works,
Full liberty to enter—stroll about;
  Much less of *red-tape* with official clerks,
So far, their freedom shows beyond a doubt.
  The Representatives of other realms,
May learn a lesson from this freedom shown.
  Where is the danger? they may ask themselves,
Of having strangers' galleries larger grown,
Accommodating thus constituents of their own?

D

XVI.

In Senate-House, and in the Congress too,
The members freely act in all their musters;
   And dress as suits convenience.   Not a few
Wear,—if the heat is great,—plain nankeen-dusters.*
   The energetic, ardent men, in both
The legislative floors enforce their will,
   Like statesmen elsewhere; often times an oath
Will crown a climax.   Thus they oft fulfil
Constituent pledges with a diplomatic skill.

XVII.

Each member of the Legislative corps
Has elbow room, with desk, and ink, and pen,
   Abundant passage room upon the floor;
Large galleries for diplomatic men.
   The speaker's chair is raised upon a dais;
Official porters guard its ins and outs;
   The ladies,—black and white,—have ample space
To keenly watch the orator that spouts.
The freely-speaking press, decides his hopes and doubts.

* Thin Nankeen coats.

XVIII.

The lantern and the dome, inside and out,
While Congress sits, are lighted up with gas;
  Electric wires circle them about;
Instant connection, and the lightning has
  Changed breath of coal into a brilliant blaze.
The gallery which high surrounds the dome,
  Draws to the willing eye, the city's-maze,
With streets so broad,—there is no lack of room,
The " Potomac " is marked by distant steam-boat fume.

XIX.

Now Baltimore in Maryland is South;
So there, in some hotels, are waiters black,
  With grinders white, set in extensive mouth.
Being now free,—observe you do not lack
  Politeness in your orders ! Then, they'll serve
What you demand with great alacrity.
  Appellatives familiar—no reserve,—
Will gain their hearts in every southern city;
Blunders are frequent, so are excuses witty.

xx.

Columbia, herself, is lady-like;
Each of her daughters hopes she is the same;
    For salary's sake they very often strike,
No matter what their colour, what their name.
    Dinah is free like " Missus," so, assumes
All the fine airs for ladies' imitation;
    In left-off clothes she struts, and grins, and fumes,
Amongst her sable friends,—a grand sensation!
High heels, projecting stern, her hair in elevation.

xxi.

Necessity, the mother of invention,
Has taught Columbia many novelties,
    To save the cost of labour,—the intention.
Thus, railway cars run with the greatest ease
    Through all chief streets in all her numerous towns,
And at a cost that does not overtax
    The neediest rider.   Still, this keeps not down
The monstrous charge for transport by their hacks!
A dollar for shilling rides, much of imposture smacks!

XXII.

The Yankee enterprise is not outdone;
'Twill well compare with any live or dead;
For them great wealth this energy hath won;
The aim of life with them is " go a-head."
In Europe primogeniture has caused
Rich families their hoards to pile on pile;
But in the States the Yankees have not paused
To spend it in great works, and yet, meanwhile,
To follow Fashion's lead in the true Paris style.

XXIII.

Wide streets, long avenues, and hotels vast,—
Big river boats,—blocks of palatial stores!
Ambition leads them on so very fast.
Though a mere infant, yet that infant soars
On eagles' wings, an eagle's height to gain,
Amongst the proudest nations of the earth.
Aye! and 'tis likely she'll her seat retain.
To what inventions she has given birth!
The telegraph and rail each year augment her worth.

XXIV.

Commerce, the offspring vast of Enterprise,
Of Wealth herself the parent has become;
  Wealth marries Luxury, and thence arise
Taste, Art, and Science.   Not yet all, but some
  Of the refinements Intellect creates,—
Known to old world long centuries ago,—
  Are now possessed by cities in the States;
And will, as Education marches, grow
To very large proportions. The future this will show.

XXV.

Music, with Ballet, at their Opera House;
Their Galleries of Art good talent show;
  And patriotic hymns their ardour rouse.
Their clubs, or "circles," strangers like to know.
  Theatres they have, where histrionic kings
Strut on the boards, as upon Europe's stage:
  A peal of bells from sacred steeple rings.
In Literature they have adorned the page
Of Science, Poetry—Mechanics is their rage.

XXVI.

Fine squares and parks,—the Central Park, to wit,
And Fairmount Park in Philadelphia;
In Baltimore, their "Druids' Hall" is fit
With Europe's pleasure-grounds the palm to share.
A "Crystal Palace" is about to vie
With Sydenham's glorious courts—of Kent the pride:
Like "Prospect Park,"—still in their infancy.
But time will beautify each drive and ride: [them wide.
Good taste has planned the whole, and wealth has made

XXVII.

But human institutions at the best
Must be imperfect. The United States
Mourns its Republic's faults. But still, the test
Is scarce a century old. Though, should the Fates
Not be adverse, Columbia will yet
Apply the besom, sweep state-stables clean,
Place men in power, where intellect is met
By patriotic worth—not shoddies mean;
Then will the glories of the Stars and Stripes be seen!

XXVIII.

Columbia of her preachers is most proud,—
Well educated, manly, eloquent.   [crowd.
    North, east, west, south, their flocks some churches
Political Religion gets full vent.
    The State is unconnected with the Church,
Which self supports.   Money is freely spent;
    Religion leaves no township in the lurch;
If need of church, the aid is given or lent;
Mistakes, of course, are made, though good is the intent.

XXIX.

Ward Beecher, of Brooklyn, well holds his own
For homely eloquence; as is the case,
    With elegance combined, in Washington,
Where Doctor Newman shines with holy face,
    And Doctor Scudder, ardent, earnest, true,
And numbers more that answer Heaven's calls,—
    A priesthood, holy in Columbia's view :—
Her zealous, active "Reverend Newman Halls,"
All pious men on whom the sacred mantle falls.

XXX.

No spectacles are needed to observe
The tear of sorrow in Columbia's eye,
When newspapers their selfish ends to serve,
For ink, use venom, when their goosequills ply
To stir up dregs of bitterness,—that's old,
On either side of the Atlantic main.
Britannia spreads her trident o'er her fold,
Tears of deep sympathy her eyelids gain,
Pressing her daughter's hand, she bids her sons refrain.

XXXI.

Brothers will quarrel, and sisters too will snap ;
"Dear ladies, don't be cross,"—you know it's true ;
But bitter strife is always a mishap,
And quite absurd, when for the selfish few.
Columbia's path is clear.—Peace is her aim,
So to develop her resources vast.
Britannia in her heart admires the fame
Her child, Columbia, gains, and prays 'twill last,
She and the world applaud successful struggles past.

XXXII.

Brave Pericles, once old Áthenë's chief,
Asserted that his son governed the world;
 And to remove his hearer's unbelief,
Argued it thus:—" My boy, whose hair is curled,
 Governs his Ma, and his Ma governs me,
I govern Athens, Athens the world doth sway :
 Ergo, my son, (it's very plain to see,)
Governs the world, and doth so in this way."
—For such misrule as this, dearly doth mankind pay.

XXXIII.

The Yankee urchin, not yet in his teens,
Imitates his dad with quid and weed;
 And, while he struts before Columbia's queens,
Asserts he's equal to papa—indeed,
 His father's good,—quite, as the President,
Who though State-servant, yet with monarchs vies :
 So the young monarch, like a somnolent,
Fancies himself a king, and vainly tries [sighs.
To extort a homage, which kings reach oft through

XXXIV.

Their Courts of Law are like the English Court;
No wig nor gown does Judge or pleader wear;
   Jury is chosen,—malice says " they're bought,"
And sell their verdicts, at the price they bear.
   Their laws are sensible, and just, and sound,—
When well administered—but otherwise,
   Justice is outraged, and the injured bound
To claim Columbia's aid. This goddess tries
To rectify abuse. How oft Columbia sighs!

XXXV.

Experience of the past has clearly shown,
In states political, there must exist
   An opposition—thus have cliques upgrown;
Which, all the human passions quick enlist
   To check corruption and extravagance.
So far, 'tis well,—but, when a venal herd
   Employs foul means in shivering its lance,—
Threatens, corrupts, and falsifies its word,—
Columbia feels the sting, and thinks her sons absurd.

XXXVI.

When such a herd as this attains to power
Through all the States, turns good officials out,
   And in their stead, puts crafty fools that lower
The robbed exchequer: then beyond a doubt,
   The Stars and Stripes lose much of man's respect,
The "outs" by thousands suffer instead of chiefs:
   Besides, the new ones work to ill effect,
And justify their plunder, laugh at griefs;   [leaves.
Helpless to heal her wounds, such field the Patriot

XXXVII.

The unespoused, sad, yet unmaidened child,
Sheds tears of bitterness she cannot stay:
   Too late, she mourns her honour so beguiled,
The priceless treasure she has thrown away.
   So, in the States, if men, just, wise, and skilled,
For party purpose, or mistaken zeal,
   Yield once to "Demos" the high posts they filled,
It is too late! "Demos" soon learns to feel
The majesty of power in the commonweal.

XXXVIII.

In every country vulgar snobs are found;
Columbia knows this well and nods assent:
But too well remembers from her native ground
Have sprung up citizens, wise, eloquent,
    Worthy, and just, and by high honour crowned;
And equalling the fine old English breed;—
    In Literature and Politics renowned,
Columbia's proud of many a "Thurlow Weed,"
To wisely guard her rights in diplomatic need.

XXXIX.

Columbia gravely pondering all this o'er;
Commands the pedagogues to spread abroad,
    And teach young Demos to respect her power,
Wise growing, with true education stored;
    And by religion rendered just and good.
This, being accomplished,—the Republic then
    May proudly love—(for first time understood,)
Their young Democracy. Then future men   [pen.
Will laud the "Stars and Stripes" with golden ink and

———

NEGRO CHURCH.

I.

THE Almighty, in His social scheme,
  Willed that the Western World
Should be aroused from slavery's dream,
  So Freedom's flag unfurled;
The Southern mind failed to foresee
  What North had felt before;
Satan obscured high Heaven's decree,
  And coaxed them into war.

II.

Few of the horrors war entailed
  Were missed by Southern States;
When retribution came, men quailed,
  And blamed the angry Fates.
Vast were the interests at stake,—
  Brothers in slavery,—
God smote the hated chain, it brake,
  And left the black man free !

III.

The black, thus freed, the law obeys,
  Accepts Religion's aid ;
Unto the white man's God, he prays :
  Some thus are serious made.
As servant, labourer, artizan,
  The whites' esteem some earn ;
And civic rights make each black man,
  With civic ardour burn.

IV.

Religion, now, to all her fanes
    The coloured race invites,
But, still, the Negro-mind refrains
    From worship with the whites.
It pleases blacks as well as whites,
    Different sects to favour :
Of bygone wrongs, and present rights,
    Their sermons often savour.

Columbia with becoming zeal,
    Strives all to educate ;
So, now, the coloured races feel
    Their influence in the state.
Some of the educated blacks,
    To preach Christ's law are called ;
And chide their flocks for conduct lax
    —Ofttimes, these stand appalled.

VI.

"My bred'ren dear! to church come near,
    While I tell of Christ's teaching;
You'll thrive 'tis clear, nor need of fear
    Unless by over-reaching!
To black and white, the "God of might"
    Will give what's just and due,
If all that's right you'll keep in sight.
    Be honest, faithful, true!

VII.

"All laws obey of States that sway
    The sceptre where you breathe,
Then God will weigh all wrongs that prey,
    And press you underneath!
So, He who tries 'midst Heaven's skies,
    To lift you from earth's scum,
Will soothe your sighs, and bid you rise
    In the Millennium!

VIII.

"It makes me grieve that I must leave,
  To preach in distant climes;
But God will weave with your belief
  Comfort for future times;
I'm going away, but there will stay
  Brud'der in orders holy:
He every day for you will pray;
  So don't be melancholy."

IX.

Sermon ended,—he descended
  From rostrum to the *dais*;
The unbefriended soon saw mended
  This break in teacher's place.
Next preacher soon prayed for a boon—
  Mounting the pulpit high:
Then 'Miss Quadroon' fell in a swoon,—
  All from a pent-up sigh!

X.

It is thought fit, the sexes sit,
   In negro Church,—apart !
That shafts of wit Sambo shan't hit
   'Gainst lubbly Dinah's heart !
This may be well, for truth to tell—
   Dinah's emotional;
She'll groan and yell, with big sobs swell—
   Hyper-devotional !

XI.

Her neighbour black gives her a smack,
   Besides a lively shake ;
To bring her back to order's track,
   And keep her soul awake :
When one shrieks out, there's little doubt,
   It others set a-going ;
Then black lips pout, while numbers shout—
   " Glory ! Glory's growing !"

XII.

Preacher well knows how all this grows,
    So calls on choir to sing :
Then " Chorus " shows, how these negroes
    The Church can make to ring !
Rare energy, black preacher-free
    Displays in all he tries ;
Their flocks this see—hence, sympathy,—
    By groans, by sobs, and sighs !

XIII.

Each Venus black good-taste may lack,
    Tho' fond of tawdry-fine ;
Gay stripes on back, good-natured clack,
    Make dusky-Dinah shine !
Black pastor next, chooses for text,
    A verse appropriate ;
To show why sects should not be vexed
    To pay the church's rate.

XIV.

" Dear bred'ren good !—it's understood,
 My younger brudder's going
'Mongst nations rude, where heavenly food
 Is very slow a-growing.
He, for your sake, well pleased, will take
 Letter, message, token,
O'er land and lake—you them must make,
 So that they won't be broken !

XV.

" While he's away, let us all pray
 That God will give him light !
With holy ray all toils repay,
 All dangers put to flight !
That Gospel true, as taught to you,
 May teach your absent friends
To keep in view what Christ can do
 For sin to make amends.

XVI.

"To God 'tis due that I ask you
 The ' building-fund ' to aid ;
Dollars—a few from every pew—
 Then Church cost will be paid.
'Tis known to all, our church is small,
 And inconvenient :
Lest harm befal this righteous call,—
 As yet—no money's spent ;

XVII.

" Nor will there be, till we can see
 Dollars two hundred more !
Then we are free !—builders agree
 At ready money score !
Blessed is such sight, that we to-night
 By bills—not ink and pen,
Each with his mite, has earned such right :
 God bless you all !   Amen ! "

———◆———

THE HUDSON.

I.

HUGE as our orb appears, yet when compared
With space that's infinite, it dwindles down.
   To a mere atom. Still Jehovah cared
To give it fire and force. So in the crown
   Of fiery Sol, it glitters as a gem.
Time hath drawn off its molten-surface heat,
   And cooled the crust to rock, thereby to stem
The ardent upbursts, that from centre meet,   [beat.
   Floods of big tears when clouds against its surface

II.

How long it is since the Plutonic force,
Did rend the earth, and thrust the hills aloft,
   As yet hath found no record in the course
Of human history! the rocks, while soft,
   As silt, and sand, and peat, and scoriæ;—
Inclosing fossils in their divers moulds;
   Which time hath hardened, Nature hath set free
On mountain summits and in sylvan wolds:—
Were hid from human ken, till science them unfolds.

III.

But now, the sequence of these changes past,
Geology expounds with Science' light;
   The fossil-glyphics are explored at last,
And tell the secrets to translators' sight.
   Thus, the Almighty in His goodness shows
How fossil expert may decipher rocks,
   Whose mystic tracing fairly well he knows;
The skeletons, entombed in mountain blocks
Are stratified at first, then raised by mighty shocks.

IV.

So, when the forces that had wrought such change
Upon the Western-World became appeased;
  Columbia was appointed to arrange
Its future destiny. Upheavals ceased,
  Enormous mountains formed the water-sheds;
And then, the grandest rivers of the earth
  Transported and spread out-alluvial beds;
Scooping deep channels. Mighty floods had birth,
And mountain-ranges grand augment their native
                                [worth.

V.

When fair Columbia took her sister's hand
That guides the merchant thro' from clime to clime,
  She pointed to her rivers, long and grand:
Commerce her chances saw, and in quick time,
  Lake wedded into river. Through the land
Cutting canals: so, joining them to seas;
  " Levees" threw up,—embankments to withstand
Erratic overflows. This at once frees.   [ease.
Large tracts of flooded land, to yield rich crops with

VL.

To Eastern States, first settled, Commerce brought
Life's necessaries;—comforts follow these.

Time, as he passed, them all experience taught;
Their many rivers speak of wealth and ease.

And so, the "Hudson," like the German Rhine,
Boasts factories, mansions, villas, on its banks,

High bluffs, tree-topped, whose branches intertwine,
Imparting beauty, as their sylvan ranks   [thanks.
Call forth Columbia's praise,—a grateful nation's

VII.

Old father Hudson has to bear the weight
Of many millions of gigantic tons

Of grain, and lumber, and all other freight—
The yield of Western and Canadian runs,

By rail and river brought to mighty lakes;
Then, thro' canals on Hudson's flood, to ride

In gallant fleets.   The saucy steam-tug makes
Their passage sure and quick, to sea outside   [pride.
Of New York harbour, which Columbia views with

VIII.

When fancy leads the tourist from New York
To mount the Hudson on a side wheel boat
   At twenty miles an hour-speed, you walk
Thro' grand saloons of an hotel afloat.
   He must, indeed, be full of Fancy's faults
Who fails to draw great pleasure from such sights,
   Excited admiration ofttimes halts,
To dwell on beauties of the Hudson's heights,
A nation's enterprise, and a free people's rights !

———•◦•———

SARATOGA.

I.

IT were unjust to blame Columbia
For introducing fashions a la mode;
But of her daughters, a great number here,
In Long Branch, Saratoga, seek abode.
During the summer, their Long Branch is—Brighton;
And Saratoga is—the Yankee Bath.
Wealth, worth, and wit, at both you may alight on;
Tho' many a spurious imitation hath
Run in the self-same groove, to follow Fashion's path.

II.

Now, Saratoga is a spot, where springs
Of mineral water from the earth do spout ;
Report (oft times a fibber) loudly sings
Their reputation, just for turning out
Diseases from the blood of bodies-human.
Taste they of sulphur, salts, and iron ? Yes—
And to the nose and tongue of lovely woman,
Would be disgusting ; but they effervesce !   [guess.
Fashion vouchsafes them good,—what follows you may

III.

" Grand Union Hotel " at Saratoga,
With its annexes, gardens, and court-yards,
Its rooms for baths, for serving tea and mocha,
Its dining-hall, already stretched upwards
Of twice one hundred feet in actual length,
Covers a site, just over acres seven.
One thousand seven hundred is the strength
Of beds prepared.   Such are the numbers given,
In the Midsummer months and full sunshine of Heaven.

IV.

More than a hundred waiters find employ;
And twice that number for all other work,—
For laundry, kitchen, baths, and for the joy
Of those who foot it to the fiddler's jerk,
Fair ladies flaunt in most expensive suits,
And change them often.   Husband has to pay!
Now this Columbia pains, because, the fruits
Of prodigal expenditure, she'll say
Are debt and fraud, and failure, in some unholy way.

V

One pays for bed and board at this hotel,
Of dollars—five per diem; this includes
All house accommodation; balls as well.
These latter are well managed—none intrude,
Without a challenge.   Hotel band is good,
Lofty and large the room wherein they dance.
Propriety is strictly understood!
Politeness, ease, and grace, so much enhance
The pleasure of such unions, meeting there by chance.

VI.

During three months, that Saratoga springs
Become the rage with our Yankee brothers;
The fat and lean, imperious Fashion brings,
With young and old, and some reluctant mothers
The face of ebony, of yellow, blond;
The sickly, healthy, active, and the halt;
To gulp down by the pint, this bev'rage fond—
Making grimaces, fit for—Epsom salt: [fault.
Fashion looks on and laughs, and thinks 'tis not her

VII.

Of course 'tis tiresome, but Beelzebub,
Either in person, or by delegate;
Will spit his venom, and his tail will rub
Against all sorts of people in a state.
He breathes in springs—they then of sulphur smell
His ardent spirits make them foam and bubble;
Blacklegs and sharpers, betting men as well,
By clinging to his tail, their risks may double—
Leaping and leaping down, to dev'lish depths of trouble.

VIII.

The ride is varied, so too, is the road
Which leads from Saratoga to Lake George,
The railway groans beneath its monster load,
Flitting thro' many a charming vale and gorge.
When done with rail, " stage " rules o'er *road of planks,*
Wood being plentiful, its use is cheap:
The introducers merit Yankee thanks:
Rough logs are placed along the way, to keep
The planking to the sod, o'er vale and mountain steep.

LAKE GEORGE.

I.

When from the summit of high mountain pass,
  One catches the first glimpse of distant lake—
Bright shining, like the light from silvered glass; [wake!
  What thoughts that slumbered, now are prone to

II.

In Popish lands, where men bow down the head,
  To that Almighty Judge that governs all,
And by the fashion of Rome's Church are led
  To prayer at Matins', or at Vespers' call.

F

III.

Their tinkling bells are heard above, below,
   Suggestive of the past ; of what's to come ;
Then, firm resolves will to our promise grow,
   When each has gained once more his quiet home.

IV.

But here, Lake George approaches to the sight,
   As " coach and four " doth o'er the planking rattle,
Passing the "Bloody Pond" where, from fierce fight,
   Sunk were the corses of those slain in battle.

V.

Much rugged, wild uncultured scenery,
   The eye encounters in this favoured spot.
Villas are few.   There is steam-machinery,
   For working mines, where such wealth can be got.

VI.

Lake George ! Columbia's justly proud of thee !
   Thy placid waters throb with gentle gales ;
The mountain zephyrs, as they crowd on thee,
   Urge on thy barks, and swell their willing sails.

VII.

Thy banks and brakes whisper of lovers' sigh;
　Thy Naiads murmur tender music strains,
Thy elfin sprites, when Cynthia mounts the sky,
　Bathe in her beams, and join in their refrains.

VIII.

Thy many miles of margin, rich appear
　With undulating mountains, choicely set
In emeralds rare.　For each day in the year,
　A separate sylvan islet will be met.

IX.

The mirrored surface of thy lake reflects
　Each cloud of angels, flitting through the skies;
As ling'ring o'er the glass, each thus inspects
　Faces celestial, and then heavenward flies.

X.

Lake House upon Lake George, as an hotel,
　Claims honourable mention.　The service good,
Better the food.　The landlord treats you well,—
　The house romantic, and the scenery rude.

XI.

Hotel, " Fort Henry William," at South End
    Of this fair lake, boasts a commanding view,
O'erlooking flood, and lovely isles which tend
    To captivate the soul and senses too.

XII.

Lake George's sister—Lake Champlain,—in size
    Is very far the greater,—still as fair,
To all that beauty love.   Her isles uprise,
    Lacustrine chieftains, crowned with verdant hair.

XIII.

Thro' both these lakes steamboats transport you fast,
    Calling at stations for exchange of freight;
Much ironstone is here, in ingots cast,
    By Vulcan's order to supply the state.

XIV.

Nature is bountiful, we're ofttimes told,
    And, certainly, this lake-district has been
Grandly turned out of Nature's finest mould,
    And clothed in raiment rich as can be seen.

xv.

As 'tis with Europe, so will it be here ;
  The emerald margins of these silver lakes,
Adorned with villa-gems, will soon appear,
  As wealth her devotees luxurious makes.

———◆———

THE ST. LAWRENCE.

I.

'TIS nearly now four hundred years ago,
Since the bold spirits of the Eastern World
    Dared the Atlantic.   Sebastian Cabot,
On Cap de Nada, the first flag unfurled,
    From Portugal and Spain, the streams went forth
Of fearless captains to the sunny South,
    Of the New Western World.   While, to the North,
The hardy sons of Gallia, fierce, uncouth, [rence' Mouth."
For Gallia, seized the realms, reached thro' "St. Law-

II.

That was a gallant time for daring crews ;
Discovery, conquest, and the thirst for gain :
   Nor high, nor lowly born, could scarce refuse
To brave the perils of the Western Main.
   Europe's best blood, aye, and forsooth, its worst,
Crowded the cruisers for the world just found :
   They vied in deed of daring ;—'twas a thirst
To plunder others' gains ; ofttimes, their ground.
Freebooters lawless, then, were by foul licence crowned.

III.

So, Canada was settled by the French,
Who held it till the " foaming-dogs of war "
   From Albion were unkennelled ; and did wrench
This land from St. Denis ; and in the claw
   Of the tridented sceptre of their brave
Britannia, who so long has ruled the main,
   Planted it firmly.   Let her rulers crave
From Heaven the right, with Justice, to maintain, [gain.
Such fiercely conquered lands, but for the conquered's

IV.

Stern Mars, tho' grey with age, is young in art
Of modern warfare.   Shield of Pachyderm,
   Or well wrought metal ;—falchion, bow and dart,
Gorget or greaves, or breast-plate, e'er so firm ;—
   Of no avail are these against the force
Invention draws from gunpowder and steam.
   Invention ! hast thou stomach for remorse,
On seeing battle fields with carnage teem ?
What worthy sequence to thy acts will this redeem ?

V.

Are the war-whisperings into monarchs' ears,
As well of those who guide the sceptred hands,
   Embroiling citizens in constant fears,
The promptings only of high Heaven's commands ?
   Those that most hate the sects that " crosses bear,"
And gloat on mortal strife, and hate so well ;
   Obeying the commands of Lucifer,
And coaxing those they prompt, his crew to swell ;
Take devilish delight with high-born souls to dwell.

VI.

As o'er the realms of earth, plain common sense
Her daily visit pays, from race to race ;
  In company with sage experience :
To all the honest, thinking men, the case
  She thus submits :—Is not the price too high,
For such protection as a despot yields ?
  A despot, in whose ears war-demons cry,
Glory ! Ambition ! Conquest ? So, he wields
War's-power unrestrained, and desolates your fields !

VII.

Did God high intellect to man impart ;
Place Nature's forces, too, within his ken ;
  Give him such power, conferred by Science, Art,
And did His Son die on the cross, for men,
  To such vile purpose, that a despot's will
Should turn tough Teutons and gay Gauls to foes—
  For an idea ? should dread artillery kill
Thousands in arms, yet powerless to close ;   [mows ?
Whilst with relentless scythe the ranks Death fiercely

VIII:

Shame to thee, Europe ! and its men of sense,
For so submitting to tyrannic will :
    Arise ! and from such hands the sceptres wrench,
And trust to others made responsible.
    Should these abuse them, fit their necks a rope.
Christ died for sinners, and for " Peace on earth."
    Remember this ! In Legislature, cope
With devilish attempts to call to birth,
The tinsel of vain glory, in place of Christian worth.

IX.

How different is war, now waged, to when
The wooden walls of Albion thundered forth
    Her flaming broadsides on the unhappy men,
She thought her foes ! Still, she protects the North,
    Of the vast Western World.   Columbia owns
Most that is South of the St. Lawrence flood.
    Each nation from the Almighty, merely loans
Controlling power.   This, when understood,
Shows that this loan divine must bear an interest good.

X.

The great St. Lawrence need, like Justice, wear
A bandage o'er his eyes, to fairly weigh
   The Southern claims of those, who proudly bear
The Stars and Stripes : as well of North, that sway
   Canadian destinies, beneath the flag,
Which Great Britannia o'er her commerce floats,
   From Western region, and high mountain crag
Descend the streams, on which St. Lawrence doats ;
Swelling in length and width, like monster giants'
                                 [throats.

XI.

The mouth of such a throat is wider far,
To let fresh out, and take salt water in,
   Than other gulfs of all America,
Whose swelling flood huge tributaries win,
   Hundreds of miles beyond St. Lawrence Gulf ;
On his left bank the famed Quebec doth stand :
   Which Albion gained, when lost was General Wolfe.
The city nestles 'neath some towering land,—
The plains of Abraham, and citadel so grand !

XII.

Fleets of sea-going boats of tonnage vast
Mount to Quebec, urged by commercial zeal;
  Exchanging freight in river-steamers fast,
Impelled by screw or quicker paddle-wheel.
  The citadel, like a grand sentry, guards
The nestling town and the broad river way.
  This town is French, more so than those upwards,
With Church and Convent,—homage, too, they pay
To Pope, tho' less just now than at a former day.

XIII.

Many a river, and majestic too,
Hundreds of miles around of upland, drains,—
  Disgorging produce : many a craft with crew,
So feeding commerce, thrives on commerce' gains.
  Town after town, settled along the banks
Of the St. Lawrence, (school for hardy tars,)
  Swells to importance in Dame Fortune's ranks.
Not quite so fast, as 'neath the Stripes and Stars, ⌈cars.
Each town employs steam-power in mills, boats, railway

XIV.

St. Lawrence' flood contracts at Montreal,
So that a bridge can span from shore to shore,
   Nearly two miles in length ; yes, and so tall,
That masts, high fifty feet, and somewhat more,
   Can pass beneath this mighty span of iron.
The Grand Trunk Railway, from Canadian side,
   Shoots through Victoria bridge so formed, to lie on
Many sustaining piers. With a just pride [the tide.
Both North and South survey this road which spans

XV.

At Montreal, Commerce is pleased to see
Such gallant fleets, and from such divers climes,
   Unloading freight upon her noble quay :
Speaking in language plain, of prosperous times.
   Fine is its market, of " le bon Secours ;"
The finest of the kind across the Main.
   Churches and Chapels—Hospitals for poor,—
The College of Mc'Gill, where youth may gain
A culture highly wrought, or education plain.

XVI.

A few miles further up, descending boats
Rush down the rapids of far famed "Lachine."
    The Indian pilot in this peril gloats,
Guiding the bark the hidden rocks between,
    Storms and tornadoes too will sometimes worry
The great St. Lawrence when he would be quiet:
    And then, his speed is here a fearful hurry,
His mighty chest upheaves with inward riot:—
The gods have willed the storm, he must obey their fiat.

XVII.

And when the monstrous streams, themselves up-
Which feed the great St. Lawrence, it may hap, [swell,
    That his contents become too large to dwell
Between his banks, and therefore from his lap
    Out flows the aqueous food to hollows fill—
So islets form; albeit, in time, they too
    Waste by attrition; and dissolve until
Their smallest disappear—leaving but few.
Repletion's very apt this flooding to renew.

XVIII.

Thus, are the islets very numerous,
'Twixt Montreal and Kingston, on left bank ;
  " The Thousand Islands " is this spot you pass :
And certainly their beauty makes them rank
  With emerald islets, elsewhere to be seen.
The eye is charmed—so rich in form and size :
  Some tenanted by trees—all clothed in green ;
Oval, or long,—or hilly, they uprise.
And Naiads nestle there with zephyrs from the skies.

XIX.

When these are passed, the grand Ontario-lake
Spreads its broad sheet—a raised, sweet-water sea ;
  Two hundred miles across.   Here, the winds make
Its troubled bosom rise defiantly.
  Waves rise o'er waves, as though great Neptune ruled;
St. Lawrence is enraged : and gusty hosts
  Expend their wrath; as troops do, when well schooled
In conflicts fierce : so, many a crew of ghosts   [posts.
Haunt their ill-fated wrecks, and guard their midnight

XX.

The margin of this lake with towns is set;
Toronto stands the chieftain of them all:
   At its broad quays rich argosies have met:
Fine "hotel-steamers" at this city call.
   Its streets are wide,—"Queen's Park" is very fine;
And "Osgoode Hall" does credit to the town.
   Its University unfolds a mine
Of literary lore and high renown
For the Canadian youth who seek high honour's crown.

XXI.

Three hundred feet below the Erie—lake,
Toronto stands upon Ontario:
   Niagara's-falls its river's burthens take
And hurl it o'er the rapids,—down below.
   Commerce, to join these lakes, applied her skill;
So Welland-Channel wide and deep was made
   With eight-and-twenty locks, to mount the hill.
St. Lawrence's full length, by easy grade,
Its produce thus confers upon the shipping trade.

CHICAGO.

I.

FOUR decades since, upon some swampy land
On Western side of broad Lake Michigan;
  Some dozen log-huts in much fear did stand
Of Indian carnage.   Here was formed the van
  Of Western forts, to guard the advancing streams
Of white-faced emigrants from Eastern clime.
  Columbia gazed thereon and musing, dreams
Of city rising up, rich, grand, sublime
In enterprising acts, achieved despite of Time !

G

II.

Sweet music rose from out the placid lake;
Its fairies were to hold a brilliant court,
    Because their queen chose, for Columbia's sake,
A city to create in fairy-sport.
    'Midst all the glitter of her queenly train,
She waves her magic wand—so, now, upgrows
    A settled township. Speculators gain
Unheard of wealth. The tide of commerce flows
Thro' lake and fifteen rails; and thus Chicago rose.

III.

But fairy architecture is not quite
The very best to meet all mortal need;
    Hygiene found its level was not right,
So, the kind fairy shook her wondrous reed.
    Straightway the streets and roads aloft were put;
Men ate, and drank, and bartered, all the while:
    Their dwellings quietly rose foot by foot:
And so, this fairy with her queenly smile,
Bade grand Chicago rise in true Columbia-style!

IV.

E'er long, bright Commerce sued the fairy-queen
To join the lake with Gulf of Mexico:
    Again the wand was waved, and straight was seen,
Betwixt the Mississipp and Chicago,
    A ship-canal, uniting gulf and lake.
Another flourish of the wand doth gain
    The railway speculators, so to make
Atlantic interests run a railway train,
Thro' grand Chicago to the great Pacific main.

V.

The fairy towards the South directs her wand—
Millions of acres'-yield of stock and grain,
    This town receives. And so, at her command,
Two thousand miles of Western produce gain
    The same depôt. This potent queen to please,
Pomona, Ceres, and Sylvanus too,
    All their vast offerings from the North release
Into Chicago's lap. Of course, it grew
Magically fast to heights, attained by very few!

VI.

But how to handle such increasing yields
Perplexed e'en Commerce.   So, her fairy kind
   Three hundred acres chose of neighbouring fields,
For a Stock-market.   This doth standing find
   For "heads," two hundred thousand at a time.
Ceres was asked, her yields in bulk, to send;
   So, " Elevators " large—in height, sublime !
Sprang from the earth, their service to extend, [vend.
All grain, in bulk they hold, to measure, cleanse and

VII.

The river's banks were insufficient found
For docks and wharves ;—so great the shipping trade !
   The fairy in the lake drew up from ground,
Some miles of "moles," (including docks)—thus made:
   And streets increased.   Bridges the river spanned:
That vehicles might pass from side to side.
   These bridges wide were upon swivels planned :
By turning these, large ships up-river ride ;
But passengers are stopped by chasm gaping wide.

VIII.

This to surmount, the little fairy-giver
Of such rare blessings, bade two tunnels straight
　To be scooped out beneath the bed of river.
The impatient fay would not allow to wait
　The mighty traffic due from East to West.
The fresh lake Michigan serves as reservoir!
　Chicago thus is served at fay's behest,—
Into " the Crib "* the limpid stream doth pour
Thro' tunnel-aqueduct, two miles at least from shore.

IX.

'Tis not quite certain what the fairy's creed is,
But it is certain, that one hundred " fanes "
　For holy worship stand ; and when there need is
Of church, of chapel still, she'll take the pains
　To make them rise, at wave of fairy-hand.
Great wealth exists wherever Commerce thrives :
　So here, the " Nine " locate, at wealth's command :
With History, Science and fine arts, each strives
Wisdom to give the men—refinement to their wives.

* Entrance to the lake-end of Aqueduct.

———◆———

REVIVAL CAMP MEETING.

I.

Who shall decide when doctors disagree
About the body's health? but, on the whole,
   Is it so sad, as when the priests we see
In hot dispute about the health of soul?
   Each of a thousand sects so firm believes
His is *the one* the Almighty most approves:
   For non-adhesion of all else he grieves;
And yet all else his own way Heavenward moves.
Will death decide for man the true Celestial grooves?

II.

Episcopalian-Methodists we find
Are very influential in the States :
  Earnest, respectable, devout, yet kind,
They hold each year a camp of delegates,
  For holy worship and for holyday.
This camp is in a forest at " Desplaines ;"
  Six leagues to Westward, on the iron-way,
From the " lake city," where queen fairy reigns.
A river skirts the camp, which thus fresh water gains.

III.

This Sylvan spot has been selected well
For " holy camp."   The trees have slender stems
  And stand apart :—the crowding-ones they fell,
The verdant grass is decked with flowery gems.
  High-growing branches meet each other's arms,
Forming umbrageous-roof, lofty, and cheap ;
  Shading the prayerful folk from just alarms
Of a sun stroke in August ; and doth keep   [weep.
The camp from being soaked, when passing clouds will

IV.

And in the midst of all, on a slight mound,
Two hundred and fifty feet across—
　Is "Circle" formed.　White houses this surround,
Whose window-sills with ornamental boss
　Shine with green paint.　So thus, a jaunty air
Is borne by streets and avenues diverging
　From the grand centre.　Canvas-tents appear,
As well in all the avenues that bring
Their occupants so earnest into this holy ring.

V.

For seats, rough planks amongst the trees are fixed
As Auditorium, a rostrum too is raised
　For purposes pastoral.　The flock is mixed
In grade and colour.　And the Lord is praised,
　With frequent "Hallelujah" and "Amen"
From deep emotion that they can't restrain,
　During the whole of prayer; and even, when
The preacher's aspirations seek to gain
The aid of Holy Ghost amongst them to remain.

VI.

Failing to come,—he begs them all kneel down,
And join with him in still more fervent prayer;
　　Some clap their hands, and shriek.　A pent-up groan
Escapes from those who fancy, or who fear
　　The Holy Ghost doth not approve their acts.
After ten minutes of this offertory,
　　The preacher seems aroused to sober facts;
He chants aloud—" I love to tell the story;"
And all the flock chime in, "O! how we live in glory!"

VII.

This camp-revival-meeting, as a rule,
Lasts for ten days in August every year;
　　It serves both holyday, and holy-school,
To all the members of this sect, that here
　　Meet distant friends from very distant parts.
Their most distinguished preachers take their turn
　　In teaching gospel, and in touching hearts.
Thus, great experience all the listeners learn;
Breathing such holy air, they all with fervour burn.

VIII.

This ten days' holiday at " Camp Desplaines "
Is inexpensive,—considered rather nice :
   A few unite, and with small surplus gains
Purchase each site, at fifteen dollars price.

   Timber abounds, so, shanties cheap upglide.
The ground floor serves both parlour and saloon :
   Above are berths, arranged so that each side
Keeps sex apart from sex ;—but friendships soon
Develop into love and then comes honeymoon.

——

NIAGARA.

I.

"THUNDER of Waters!" (great Niagara!)
The sentinel of grand St. Lawrence' stores
   Of mighty river wealth behind—so far,
And yet so high as Nature's reservoirs!
   Time hath forgot when first he saw thee stand
On the Ontario's edge—now, miles below!—
   Rolling the flood adown thy cataract grand
Into the frightened lake.   Thus, years did grow;
While rocks were gnawed away by thy unceasing flow.

II.

A hundred millions, here, of liquid tons
Leap every hour from off that rocky crest
　　Into the roaring gulf, whose thunder stuns
The too-near listener ! What a sorry jest
　　Are artificial cascades all to this !
Should the Almighty purpose choose ordain
　　That Lawrence flood shall tumble, roar, and hiss,
Till Time a thousand more of years shall gain,
Niagara's lion-throats will at Lake Erie strain.

III.

Islands and rocks, a few—near to the verge
Of these stupendous falls—as yet are spared
　　Amidst these rapids, and their bubbling surge.
On Iris Isle is Prospect Tower reared ;
　　By bridge connected with a land-side rock ;
So that weak mortals there may test the might
　　Of Heaven's work, and realize the shock
Of these tumultuous rapids by the sight—
Incessant in their roar, throughout the day and night.

IV.

Mighty Niagara gnaws the cliff away,
More in the centre than on either side;
Thus a crescentic crown of glittering spray
Surmounts his brow in full Imperial pride;
And when bright Cynthia attends his court,
Choice diamonds sparkle in his lunar bow;
And always, when the sunbeams shine in sport,
The monarch's diadem more rich doth grow:
Sapphires and rubies rare with scintillations glow.

NIAGARA'S FURIES.

I.

From the last rock but one of "Sisters' Isle,"
(Leaden the sky above, with drizzling rain ;)   [while,
   Spell-bound, with awe we gazed! the flood, mean-
Roared and howled out, like spirits racked with pain.

   These maddening rapids must be Dante's hell !
Millions of furies huddled, tortured, jammed ;
   Cursing and screeching with demoniac yell !
To teach those living, how the dead, the damned, [med.
Are scourged and worried, twisted, squeezed and cram-

II.

From every rock and tree where they could cling,
They rushed with fury back on Heaven's police :
   Five cedars on my left—once formed in ring—
Thus twisted and uptorn.   As shocks increase
   Charge upon charge is made—but all in vain ;
Trembling the rock below—the shores around :
   Columns with columns clash, and form again :
Celestial hosts come swooping at a bound,
And hurl their demon foes off the advantage ground.

III.

An elfin-bower, fit for fairy-revels,
Down from the right of third bridge may be seen ;
   Whose trees have been clung to so much by devils
In their impotent struggles—thus have been
   Uprooted and left waste.   Celestial fight,
God's vengeance just and Retribution's blow
   May here be viewed, by such as doubt His might.
Rebellious spirits, racked and tortured !—so,
Yelling, are tumbled into the abyss below.

IV.

The abyss below ! good God ! what direful screams
Gush from that fearful gulf, by mists surrounded :
Mists, mounting to mid-air—composed it seems,
Of atomies of hellish-spirits pounded.
Mortals know little of the spirit world ;
Niagara's giant genius draws aside
The veil, and shows the ghostly traitors hurled
From Heaven's domain—rebuking such as glide,
From Virtue's holy-paths to those of sin and pride !

NIAGARA'S FAIRIES.

I.

In ferry-boat on the Canadian shore,
Niagara's foaming cataract in view;
   Phœbus at back, whose slanting rays did pour
A magic incense o'er the mystic dew.
   The thread-like bridge, suspended in mid-air;
The distant music of the waterfall!
   I gazed with wonder! for they did appear:
What? why the fairies—so they will to all,
That patiently will thus upon their muses call.

II.

The tumbling flood is pounded into mist,
And sportive zephyrs carry this away.
   The fairies of the Fall cannot resist
Coquettish curtsying to the god of day.
   Sit where I sat, and watch the magic bow
Which Phœbus forms when on the mist he smiles :
   What tiny, little gossamers there show
Fantastic dancing, arch, seductive wiles—
Their filmy raiment all, in rainbow-fairy styles !

III.

   Let Phœbus frown, and then the spell is broke ;
No fairies now—nothing but cloud-like dew :
   But let him smile again—as if awoke
By the enchanter's wand, the fairy crew
   Are seen to waltz all round the " *arc-en-ciel*,"
Mounting above the bridge—down in the stream.
   They practise much, so dance extremely well :
Niagara's music is enough, 't would seem,
To regulate their step—their joyous mystic dream.

IV.

The Judge Omnipotent,—here, at the Fall
Of great Niagara,—the Furies shows,
  Scourged and bound up within its liquid pall;
Till battered into mist—which henceforth grows
  Into a fairy-ring, if but the solar rays
Can coax some gentle zephyrs to their aid;
  Then in this mist are seen the tiny fays,—
Teaching mankind how justly God hath made
The pain of demon-sin—its penalty how paid!

———◦◆◦———

LAKE SUPERIOR.

I.

HAVE you e'er sailed on Lake of Michigan ?
Passed thro' the charming strait of " Mackinaw ?"
 Your mind make up while I show how you can
Spend a delicious week, with scarce a flaw
 To mar your high enjoyment. Gain the boat,
" City of Madison " named. Secure a berth,
 Boat is fair sized, and knows well how to float.
Say boat or rail ? 'tis water *versus* earth.
Leisure the lake affords with ease and cheerful mirth.

II.

The boat itself is clean—saloon is smart—
Berths and beds proper— yes, and large enough
    In the staterooms ; which, too, sustain their part
For being well appointed. Not more rough
    Are the crew here, than other craft that steams.
They are civil all—the waiter is polite ;
    The captain, Davis, knows his work it seems,
And skilfully conducts the vessel right,
Keeping all things in order—cheerful, trim and tight.

III.

The steward is competent—the *menu* good.
Tables are spread with an artistic eye,
    No murmuring impatience lest the food
Should disappear too fast.—The helps all try
    To make things pleasant.—So, the chambermaid
Tho' black in face is fair in all her work ;
    And with good humour follows up her trade.
The engineers, the mates, also the clerk,
Prove by their willing acts, that duty they don't shirk.

IV.

In this, there's no mistake.   The "Madison"
In all is well appointed;—so, the sail
   From grand Chicago, up so quickly grown,
Thro' Michigan Lake, methinks will rarely fail
   To give you satisfaction quite complete.
How much more worthy this for all concerned,
   Than the gross treatment, which a friend did meet
From the "Maine" steamer, that has justly earned
The character of cheap to very nasty turned.

V.

Therein the food was bad.   Service to match.
Crowded much more than is allowed as just;
   A seat at table quite difficult to catch:
The boat was left by several in disgust;
   Two men turned sixty ousted from their bed
For a fresh comer and her children twain.
   Displeasure thus was from discomfort bred—
Obliged to quit and pay a fare again,—
Columbia frowns on thee, thou very dirty "Maine."

VI.

Thus with the " Madison " all goes cheerily,
As she glides o'er the bosom of the lake :
The golden orb shines on us merrily,
Whilst Cynthia from her face the veil doth take,
Racine, Milwaukee, Sheboygon, and all
The other stopping points we reach and land—
Pass thro' the straits.—At Mackinau we call,
The isle of Blois-blanc sight on our right hand—
Lake Huron's sentinel so verdant, yet so grand !

VII.

Lake Huron kissed by gentle zephyrs' lips,
Lifts her fair bosom in responsive sighs ;
The barque, like swan enamoured, ofttimes dips
To gaze in mirror at reflected skies.
Three thousand islands set in emerald green,
Like giant-gems stand out above the lake ;
Where its gold edges have contracted been—
Forming the river Sioux.—The name they take
From Indians of that tribe, fierce yet of sturdy make.

VIII.

So saucily the " Mad'son " steams her way,
From lake, through river and these lovely isles :
  The treach'rous " Nebish " bids our vessel stay,
Till other craft have passed in single files.
  The passage being narrow 'tween the rocks,
Great care and skill in piloting you need,
  T' avoid this Scylla, who with envy mocks
The stranded bark.   Our captain takes good heed
To evade the monster, and to elude his greed.

IX.

Two hundred years have gone, since De la Salle,
A chevalier of France, built the first boat,
  To sail on lakes above Niagara's Fall.
Primeval forests formed the sylvan coat,
  All from the mountain peaks to the lake shore :
And then these forests' lords were Indians red—
  Fishing, the chase, and the pursuit of war—
Bow, arrow, shield, and knife to scalp the dead ; [tread.
Where once their wigwams stood now do the Saxons

X.

Under the red man's sway, or rather strife,
Age passed o'er age,—all was at a stand.
    Their hellish warwhoops and their scalping knife
Shut progress and improvement from the land.
    Thus from the past the future may be guessed;
Had not Columbus and his daring train
    Gone with their reckless followers to the West,
The transatlantic continent to gain,
Just savage as it was, so would it still remain.

XI.

That Power sublime the Universe that made,
And studded Cosmos with its glittering stars,
    Commanded solar systems, and forbade
Departure from his fiat,—so nought mars
    His grand creative scheme.   Emanations
Incessant from the seething orb of day
    Have gathered into nebulæ;—stations
Assign'd to them, eccentric parts to play,
As cometary wanderers in the ethereal way!

XII.

Huge heaps of cometary nebulæ
Their orbs contracted as past time rolled on ;
　　Condensing with concentric energy
To planets primal,—so reflective shone.
　　This change, from nebular to primary,
Caused masses of themselves off to be hurled,—
　　Attendant satellites, thus doomed to flee
After their leaders through the solar world,
Till God's arresting signal shall become unfurled.

XIII.

Or they together, in their spiral way,
Their orbs contracting, in the time to come,
　　Shall rush once more into the "god of day,"
And find what once they had—their future home,
　　There to submit to the consuming test !
What finite minds can in such things decide ?
　　Things infinite, which only God knows best—
Omnipotence, that o'er all worlds doth ride,
And gave His only Son, as pattern for our guide !

XIV.

Under Christ's banner then the seal is set,
The white man's task is to subdue the red,
  But Christ taught Charity ; therefore 'tis best
To deal with justice, as the Saviour said ;
And give the savage what is opportune—
By good example to be denizened.
  Such mission—grand and holy—is a boon
Unto the giver, as to him that owned   [throned.
The mighty lands from which he has been thus de--

XV.

Columbia's lands and these majestic lakes,
Or inland seas which form so grand a chain ;
  Commerce has given for our Christian sakes,
Unto Columbia.   Let her avoid the pain
  Which follows from abuse, and use it well.
Thousands of masts upon her waters ply,
  Exchanging freight with every town and port :
Columbia's banners on their summit fly ;
And now the Stars and Stripes flaunt bravely in the sky.

XVI.

In eighteen hundred and eighteen as well,
" Walk in the water "—such the name of boat—
    Was the first urged by steam—so histories tell,
Upon Columbia's inland seas to float.
    Floating-hotels now crowd this chain of lakes,
So great the freight of man and merchandise;
    Some fifteen hundred miles the distance makes
From Gulf St. Lawrence as the lakes uprise;
Mounting to Lake Superior in the cool clear skies.

XVII.

Superior Lake ! thou well deserv'st that name,
Thy high position and enormous size;
    Thy bracing air, for health hath gained thee fame,
Thy large and lovely islands, which uprise
    Like emerald bosses on a silver shield.
Thy bold and pictured rocks, thy mountain mines
    Which so much iron and rich copper yield,
Thy sylvan groves of cedar, maple, pines
Down to the water's edge, in undulating lines !

XVIII.

I have surveyed thy surface, when as clear
As townlike lady's polished toilet-glass ;
   Have seen Aurora in the east appear,
And step aside to let Apollo pass ;
   And as he urged his chariot up the sky,
His golden beams reflected in thy face,
   Pass o'er the heavenly vault, and by and bye
Sink in the western deep, with such a blaze
Of glorious refulgence as well charmed the gaze.

XIX.

I have seen thy expanse in ripples rise,
From blithesome zephyrs frolicking thereon ;
   With goat's-hair filmy clouds draping the skies,
And gull and loon, which ever and anon
   Breasted their plumage in thy gentle wave,—
These mimic waves parting before our prow
   In foaming ridges, the ship's side to lave ;
The pliant barque curtseys a little now,
And then with jaunty air essays a graceful bow.

XX.

And I have viewed thee when lashed into rage
By winds belligerent from Boreas sent,
   Although Superior, thou could'st not assuage
Thy righteous passion, but allowed it vent,
   Tossing thy surface into waves as large
As royal Neptune's grand Atlantic swell;
   With fury foaming to repel the charge
Of Boreas and his myrmidons as well;
Till mighty Jove, indignant, sought the strife to quell.

XXI.

The Olympian monarch sent his thunder-bolt
Through the arched canopy, which lightning blazed;
   Peals of artillery from heaven were rolled,
Till both the struggling winds and flood, amazed,
   Desisted for a time to gather strength.
The winds fell back, to rally leaders round—
   Augmenting for the charge in length and breadth;
With shrieks, with screams and yells, dash with a bound,
And drive the angry waves on the lacustrine ground.

XXII.

Stunned for a moment, the waves once more recoil;
With deafening roar now rush upon their foes;
  The swelling, foaming columns seek to foil
The gusty host.   So Jove doth interpose,—
  Clap after clap is rolled along the spheres,
The forked lightning turns night into day:
  And timid women shrink within with fears;
And hail, in torrents sent its part to play,
To quell this bootless strife and chase the foes away

XXIII.

Such fearful strife inflicts on mortals harm,
For ships afloat are tempest tossed and wrecked;
  And friends at home are tortured with alarm,
Before the gods the mischief can have checked.
  The angry night keeps down below the east,
Whilst the young dawn with milder aspect smiles;
  The troubled waves not yet will be appeased,
Still roll each other up in crested piles,
That rock the ship they bear for very many miles.

XXIV.

The Superior journey ends at Fond-du-Lac;
The week throughout the lakes has charming been;
　Its health-inspiring air sent many back
To enjoy its breeze and the delightful scene.
　So now we quit the vessel, which in sooth
Has bravely done its work for all concerned.
　The embryo town we reach is called Duluth,
Just one year old; in ten years 'twill be turn'd
Into a famous city, wealthy, fine, and learn'd.

XXV.

Its present boast, if any, sure will be—
Much sand and mud, and roads all broken up;
　Shanties on swamps, wigwams and squaws you'll see.
With many a barber and a liquor shop.
　Yet still it has a lake and three railways;
Its streets are laid out wide, and straight, and long,
　Four churches built; and Expectation says,
That in the future (though she may be wrong)
Its streets with very wealthy citizens will throng.

XXVI.

Duluth by rail is linked unto St. Paul,
Through scores of miles of wilderness of pine,
  Through which the Indian and wild beast did crawl,
Until the white man, by permit divine,
  Forced through this sylvan vast the iron-way,
Strode over ravines with colossal bridge,
  Swamps choked, and mighty viaducts did lay,
Access to gain to many a mountain ridge,   [sedge.
Through tangled brake and briar, and feathery fern and

UPPER MISSISSIPPI.

I.

"FATHER of floods!" those who have sailed on thee
Have seen such sights only Columbia's land
   To travellers can display. The gnarled tree
In every varied form is here at hand;
   Hanging o'er bounding stream from sylvan wood;
Crowded with elm and oak and clustering vine;—
   Stern foresters which have for ages stood,
Their ancient arms so firmly intertwine;
Its growth of underwood meets little of sunshine.

II.

The Mississippi river at St. Paul
Is distant from the sea two thousand miles,
　Its length above, thro' many a charming fall
Runs on four hundred more. As for its isles,
　With such rich verdure clad—they're numberless !
Its valley drains the largest watershed
　In the United States ;—so you may guess,
By what a host of mighty rivers fed
Is this vast flood of which so much is writ and said.

III.

Time was, tho' now indefinitely past,
When the earth's central and still raging heat
　Vented its ardour, and the hills upcast ;
Uprose the Rocky Mountains, and high seat
　Of Alleghanny and Nevada range.
The ocean's breast warmed by Apollo's smile,
　Breathed forth its vapours ; nor less true than strange
Myriads of zephyrs with seductive guiles,　　[piles.
Espoused and bore their brides to tops of mountain

IV.

Here was their ardour cooled. They melted down
To vapoury mists, to snow, to hail, and rain;
Streamlets uniting,—into rivers grown,
As Mississippi,—so the sea regain.
This vast, this lovely, this majestic vale,
Was once the empire of the Indian red;
Whose savage instincts could do nought but fail
Of man's high mission. He loved war instead,
And its barbarian treatment of the quick and dead.

V.

To thee, Columbia! the Almighty giver,
Of these vast states, these mountains, prairies, isles,
Extensive seaboards, harbours and each great river
Has them donated. And now its surface smiles
With commerce and her sisters,—Science and Art.
Rivers by bridges spanned, and railway-cars
In cities, villages;—in every part!
Piers, docks and shipping manned by hardy tars,
That love their Fatherland—its many stripes and stars.

VI.

The passage steamers of the Mississipp'
Are built in storeys six. First is the hold,
  O'er which is "maindeck"—the whole length of ship
Covered by " grand saloon," whose doors unfold
  To lateral cabins, for sleeping or repose ;
On this again is deck called " hurricane ; "
  The " Texan " deck upon the latter grows ;
The sixth and last, the " Canopy," you gain,
Where skilful pilot holds his undisputed reign.

VII.

He need be skilful ; for the shifting bed,
Its many sandbanks, and its ugly snags
  Solicit, when the river is ill fed,
Th' arrest of unsuspecting barque, which lags ;
  Till by the lifting spars and ropes astern
They raise her bow ; then by the paddle wheel
  They wriggle, sidle, till success they earn,
Freeing the hull and the adhering keel ;
Then onward dash again, which motion soon you feel.

VIII.

The " Alexander Mitchell,"—so was named
This Mississippi's river omnibus :
    Its crew—some thirty negroes—freed and tamed,
Quarrel good-humouredly, and swear and " cuss : "
    Ragged and rollicking, good-natured, free,
Dirty and juicy, with an oily mouth ;
    'Midst their hard work, they shout and sing with glee.
Till recently in bondage by the South,
In spite of all their faults, Columbia knows their worth.

IX.

Columbia's mighty empire is so vast,
Its towns and cities up like mushrooms rise.
    The world considers Yankees very fast ;
In laying out their towns they're surely wise.
    Determine where the next township shall be,
The owners give the land, with right good will,
    For roads, for street, and church. Ere long you'll see
A town laid out with engineering skill.
Its value raised thereby does thus their purses fill.

x.

Columbia in her zeal for Yankee land,
Has summoned to her counsels Science, Art ;
   These, in obedience to her high command,
Bring skill and labour in to play their part ;
   Their strong companions—iron and steam—attend
On prairie, forest, meadow, sea and lakes :
   Nature's productions to their will they bend :—
The railways shriek, the dormant forest wakes ;
And so, the giant Steam old Neptune's region shakes.

xi.

'Ere starting from St. Paul, a captain's corse,
By guard of honour with a funeral dirge,
   Was brought on board ; many who mourned his loss.
(While his sad toll the steamer's bell they urge,)
   Removed the dead man's body at " Dubuque."
The while the brazier, with its red glare light,
   Cast on the scene a sad and mournful look.
Knell followed knell, 'till mourners out of sight ; [night.
And then the gallant ship steamed on throughout the

XII.

Early one morn the good ship got aground;
And for five hours stuck there by the sun;
   Many manœuvres tried to get her round,
All of which failed until they rigged up one
   Of starboard lifting-spars to raise her bow:
Ropes from her stern, stretch far away to shore;
   The signals whistle, and the steam-throats blow;
The vessel rolls and rocks, the engines roar,
And with a mighty strain, the steamer's carried o'er.

XIII.

At night, sometimes we stayed beside a wood,
Where lumber was collected for the boat;
   The crew of blacks their business understood;—
The bringing of logs from shore.   Each naked throat
   Swelling with ribald fun, as they between
The forest trees passed quick in single file.
   The flaring braziers' glare cast on the scene
Effects dramatic.   Buccaneers in style—
Like sable bandits each with a rich booty's pile.

XIV.

Before Christ's throne, Justice had pleaded long
The negro's plaint, nor pleaded it in vain:
Columbia blushed—acknowledged it was wrong,
And nobly broke the black man's wretched chain.
Equality did next Columbia pray
For citizen's rights: Columbia knit her brow,
And Justice stared.   At length they both gave way,
The blacks and whites have equal rights just now,—
Religion blessed this act which tyranny did cow.

XV.

From St. Paul's city unto Clinton Town,
The banks of Mississipp' are beautiful!
High hills for borders, oft to mountains grown,
Covered with foliage rich, and rare, and cool.
At frequent intervals, townships aspire
Where passengers and freight are interchanged.
Big cords of wood received for furnace-fire,
This wood in piles on the main deck is ranged;
So cheap is timber here, that coal becomes estranged.

XVI.

And then huge lumber-rafts are toiled along;
Ofttimes by steam tugs, and sometimes by oars,
   Thousands of dollars risked if aught goes wrong,
Or raft should break up on account of flaws.
   Should raft so break, the raftsman has the skill
To man a boat and bring the truants back;
   'Tis difficult, but money gains their will,
The raft once more to form,—despite a crack,— [stack.
And guide to Southern wharves, in lumber yards to

XVII.

   Three days so passed, we stop at Clinton town;
After five hundred miles of river life,
   This city young, not yet is fully grown:
Still for the future is with promise rife.
   After hotel, one seeks the river's side,
To lave the body in this mighty stream;
   'Tis at some risk—its current, like a tide,
Is dangerous as Jordan's, it would seem
Where many bathers drown, t'awake in Hades' dream.

XVIII.

Bed at hotel is change just for one night ;
For while the stars are brilliant in the sky,

   You're roused, whilst dreaming of your western flight.
Orion, yes e'en Sirius is high.

   Such facts are noted as you gain the rail ;
For Chanticleer as yet has failed to crow.

   You're westward flying, e're the east is pale :
Miles upon miles of prairie come and go ;   [grow.
Fringed is the line with gold, where now sunflowers

THE FAR WEST.

I.

COLUMBIA once with the high gods debating,
   Received a hint, how she her sons might serve,
So down to earth she came, nor long was waiting,
   To call Adventure, Enterprise, and Nerve.

II.

" Exhaustless wealth is in the far, far west;
   Go there,—make skilful survey.   Quick! report."
The sisters three, sped off at her behest
   O'er prairie, valley, mountain to sea-port.

III.

They skillfully surveyed, and straight returned,
　　Stated their views—Columbia gave command.
The sisters three, with generous ardour burned,
　　So called in Commerce to enrich the land.

IV.

The gods approved—so now the four combined,
　　The ironway is laid from sea to sea;
Valleys explored,—the snow-topped mountains mined,
　　The " Stripes and Stars " flaunt out there gallantly.

V.

But what a glorious boast for Stripes and Stars
　　To span three thousand miles from shore to shore :
Food, sleep, and elegance in Pullman's cars,
　　Unite with safety, speed unknown before !

VI.

The red man, buffalo, and bear, are now
　　Upon the iron-way but rarely seen ;
The antelope, and elk, sometimes I trow,
　　The prairie chicken, and the prairie chien.

VII.

Columbia proud of both her rail and boat,
   Could give to Europe many a useful notion,
The grand hotels which on her waters float,
   And Pullman's cars, which merit high promotion.

VIII.

Here are all comforts tourists can desire,
   For sleeping, feeding, lounging, or the weed;
Wider than Europe's, and the ceilings higher,
   In summer, cooled—in winter, warmed if need.

IX.

Just as the stately bark thro' ocean calm,
   Glides smoothly on, dashing aside the spray,
So for a thousand miles without alarm,
   O'er prairie land, one glides on iron way.

X.

At frequent stations mushroom towns spring up,
   Which will ere long to wealthy cities grow;
All the hotels provide—to dine and sup:
   Soldiers encamped—are met with oft below.

XI.

Now, Sherman on the Rocky Mountain range,
   Eight thousand feet is raised toward the sky,
Indian, Chinese, and many people strange,
   Are met or passed as o'er the earth you fly.

XII.

The valley passed, a thousand miles at least
   Betwixt the Rocky and Nevada tops :—
High up four thousand feet, the eye can feast
   On rocks contorted, in rich varied crops.

XIII.

The states Nebraska and Dacotah passed—
   The monster train glides into state Utah ;
Whose "Wahsatch" mountains, high have been upcast;
   Their passes ledged, to serve the steam-tugged car.

XIV.

This ledge, with rail winding the rocks between,
   Cut down and fixed by thrifty Mormon-hands ;
From " Observation car " is better seen—
   Romantic, picturesque ! as Alpine lands.

XV.

Deep in the gulche,* " Bear " river rolls along :
  Yonder is " Pulpit-rock " on dexter side,
Where " Weber's " spirits preach and drive the throng
  Of Wahsatch† demons, down the " Devils' slide !"§

XVI.

'Midst these contorted bluffs, the view is grand !
  Less so than" Via-Mala's " gorge, by far ;
The " thousand-mile-tree," here is left to stand,
  To show the distance west from Omaha.

XVII.

The snorting monster rolls the train along
  Thro' the Nevada to the *coast range* rocks ;
Rich, charming features on the vision throng ;
  Mountains are piled in wild enormous blocks.

XVIII.

Hard toiling miners, in rude strength and health,
  —Saxon, and Celt, and Yankee blood, commixed.
The mountains here abound in mineral wealth,
  Where aqueducts and mills have long been fixed.

---

* A ravine with water course.   † A mountain range.
§ The top of a rock so shifted as to lie obliquely.

XV.

The Sacramento gained by railway train,
　Thro' rocks, and dells, and vales, and forests vast,
The anxious eyeballs for the ocean strain ;
　And San Francisco town is reached at last.

SAN FRANCISCO.

I.

In the earth's history, but so long back,
That e'en Conjecture says, she'll "give it up,"
    Pluto received command the bonds to slack
Which bind the coast-range rocks,—so form a cup.
    Its greatest length is sixty miles, they say.
The impatient ocean was not long to wait—
    At once rushed in.   Thus San Francisco Bay
Joined with Pacific at the Golden Gate;
Here Neptune holds his court in regal pomp and state.

II.

'Many a rock erects its head on high,
And towers up above the liquid bay;
So many gulls and pelicans are nigh
To hide such surface from the solar ray.
The Goat, the Angel, and the Alcatraz,
Three famous isles selected by the State,
Are used for garrisons. The latter has
Custodian powers o'er the Golden Gate;
With guns defiant bristling: also its "Angel" mate.

III.

The great Pacific rolls its big waves in;
When Neptune's angry, they are oft uncouth:
The narrow entrance passed, they flatten thin;
And thus the bay keeps placid, calm, and smooth.
Ships of all sizes, and from every clime,
With ferry-boats three-storeyed, there abound;
Docks, wharves, and spires in so short a time
Have sprung from out the bay. On this new ground
Now warehouses, and streets, and market-ways are found.

IV.

Viewed from the boat, approaching San Francisco,
The neck of land on which the town you gain
　　Stretches from south to north.　The tide doth flow
Twice daily from the great Pacific main.
　　Back from the shore the city mounts on high,
With streets right-angled, climbing up the hills :
　　Each clean white house set in a turquoise sky
With admiration the beholder fills !
And its salubrious clime great cheerfulness instils.

V.

And when old Time approved that Enterprise
Should lead her votaries to this land of gold,
　　And wash the granite soil ; then rich supplies
Of glittering dust fell to the daring, bold
　　Mining enthusiasts from distant climes.
In '48 two hundred houses rose
　　On the bay-margin.　These in after times
Were shut out from the shore, when Commerce chose
To bid the sea retire, and broad quays interpose.

VI.

This glorious bay makes San Francisco town
The port of California, and its chief
    Pacific Ocean city of renown.
Nine miles it covers—and the time as brief
    As infant needs to gain majority,
Of souls a million's fifth it now can boast.
    All sorts of creed find homage in this city.
Ere long 'twill reach to the Pacific coast;
It joins the east and west by telegraph and post.

VII.

Mason, Oddfellow, Romanist, and Jew,
With Protestants of every tint and shade,
    Striving to gain command. The Chinese too
Have set up temples, and compete for trade
    In handicraft and every kind of toil.
When dead, their corpses in fit tombs are laid,
    For future transport to celestial soil;
For life—not death—their home they here have made.
The Irish hate them well and threaten oft a raid.

VIII.

In Art Dramatic they are much behind;
In acrobatic business they excel.
What was a Christian fane, the Chinese mind
Hath changed to Thespian temple, where they tell
Historic legends in barbaric style.
Nor scenery nor proscenium do they show;
The orchestra produces music vile;
Fiddles and gongs in deafening ardour grow;
And as the climax nears, still harder is the blow.

IX.

Celestial Thespians mince and mouth and whine,
Much like the Arab knaves at Jericho;
And oft to audience will their heads incline,
Until with mimic frenzy fierce they grow:
Then he who's doomed to lose his precious head,
Bursts from his bonds, and with a wooden sword
Lays right and left. They tumble as if dead;
Then scramble up, and bolt with one accord: [plaud.
" Ching-Fous " look on and smile, but never once ap-

x.

After some interval those that were dead
Strut in again to sound of deafening gong;
  Each gives a spring, and turns heels over head:
This fun is well sustained by motley throng.
  Sideways and backwards go the summersaults,
Until celestial wind begins to fail:
  Little it boots if merits or if faults:
Ching's features are as stolid as his tail:
Small cigarettes they make, and then the smoke inhale.

xi.

Planked road and footways stretch out mile on mile;
The dust swells into clouds in each suburb;
  And western zephyrs heap this pile on pile
Against foot pavements, in the place of kerb.
  And here, while summer lasts, the mournful clouds
Refrain from weeping. Oft a misty veil
  Enwraps the city as with funeral shrouds:
When Pluto's fires below, themselves regale,
Then earth and temples shake, and timid mortals quail.

XII.

Grand is the view from the "lone mountain" height!
The boundless main extending to the west!
 Below—"Cliff House." 'Neath this, a goodly sight,
Giving to Tourist—novelty for zest;
 "Seal Rocks" uprise abruptly from the deep,
Well clothed with " sea-dogs" of a monstrous size,
 That bask in sunshine—hold converse and sleep—
A curious spectacle for strangers' eyes   [cries.
To watch these ocean-brutes and hear their plaintive

XIII.

Now, turn the gaze towards the tropic band,
Which in mid-day is steeped in golden beams;
 The tortuous, but high, aspiring land
Kisses the sky. And, at its feet, it seems
 As if the wave in undulating lines
Dwindled by distance, to the horizon joined
 The vaulted arch unto the sea's confines.
So distance, from the rocks, their height purloin'd:
Nearer, they held the vault as clust'ring columns groin'd.

XIV.

Turn to the spot, where Phœbus mounts the skies :
Below—the city, and its glorious bay ;
Beyond—the " Coast-range " hills proudly uprise
Like giants marshall'd for a hostile fray.
"Monto Diabolo " o'ertops them all ;
His hair is hoary where the sun can't reach :
Again beyond—are ranges still more tall :
Beneath—on shore opposed—on the bay-beach
Townships are growing fast, with docks and piers to each.

THE YOSEMITE VALLEY.

I.

ERE yet Aurora had removed her veil,
Or the still lazy equerries of the sun
    Had rubbed their drowsy eyes, the east now pale,
The royal steeds whose duty 'twas to run
    O'er the arched vault, yoked to Apollo's car,
Still rested from the toil of day just passed.
    The azured roof, yet lit with moon and star :
The weary tourist held in slumbers fast,
Is waked from travel's dreams to travel's claims at last.

II.

In this new township, in this forest wild,
All was tranquillity save croak of frog,
  The rustling of the leaves, and buzzing mild
Of insect-homes in the decaying log.
  The crackling whip foretold the stage was nigh.
The bill discharged,—the coach is on its way ;
  O'er narrow road, now low, now mounting high;
Causing our jolted seats and limbs to pay,
The smarting penalty, when traveller's parts they play.

III.

Fatigue had pressed the eyelids down with lead ;
The weary limbs petitioned for repose ;
  The o'er worked senses signed it for the head,
And claimed some respite ere the journey's close.
  At Bronson's Meadows a log-hut hotel
Afforded a rough couch with meats and drinks ;
  The judgment felt the claimants had done well,
So stretched on bed, and took the forty winks, [methinks.
Which those who are travel-worn will much applaud

IV.

Sweet is such sleep, nor time enough allowed
For drowsy imps to settle in the brain;
　The fancy wakes, which down before was bowed,
And the five senses spring to life again.
　Just as the electric spark will fire cause,
So does the magic influence of sleep
　Restore brain energy, which straightway pours
The vital forces thro' the nerves, that keep　　[creep.
Healthy the sanguine streams, which through all tissues

V.

The limbs no longer weary, feel refreshed;
The mind like bow fresh strung, elastic grows;
　The senses quicken, being now unmeshed,
And note the giant trees in stately rows.
　Many are prostrate like huge skeleton,
Leviathans with their blanched vertebræ,
　Sustaining limbs whose carcases are gone:
Others are prone, whose branches you may see
As legs of centipedes, upholding trunk of tree.

VI.

The Indian fires and the white man's need,
Have turned to charcoal many a sturdy trunk;
By slow decay, or the wild tempest's greed,
These giant firs have withered and have shrunk.
And when the woodman's axe, or lightning's blast,
Cracks their supporting base, their tottering tops
Are downwards on the other giants cast; .
With frightful crash some other giant drops,
And boughs and branches fall in oft increasing crops.

VII.

Their cloud aspiring summits when they fall,
Tear from the earth their gnarled and twisted trunks;
These standing high, in misty eve, appal—
As animals grotesque, or hooded monks,
Or serpents coiled, ready to dart their fangs;
Or Indians crouching with their guns abreast:
The timid see the flash and hear the bangs;
The brave push on and laugh: for no unrest
Arrests their enterprise, or checks their trav'lers' zest.

VIII.

The horse you ride is fair, the saddle good;
Mile after mile is monster forest passed:
  Trees which for half a thousand years have stood,
O'er winding paths, their grateful shadows cast.
  The trail—the Indian trail—thro' bush and rock
Is difficult, not dangerous to go:
  Altho' 'tis difficult it does not shock
One half so much as that to Jericho—
Worn for four thousand years by horse hoof to and fro!

IX.

This trail on rocky ledge is worn.   You'll see
Foot prints of many hoofs and grisly bear;
  The mountain-cliffs of the "Yosemite,"
Break on the ravished sight as one draws near!
  The vale of the Yosemite in view;
Its trees, its meadows, and its mountains high,
  The "Merced" river, and the sky—so blue.
With "Inspiration Point," comes long-pent sigh,
Which souls poetic feel, when wonders draw so nigh.

X.

As o'er the vale you gallop on your steeds,
The silver-threaded "Merced" widens out ;
"Cathedral Rock," on dexter side one heeds,
And on the left—"El Capitan." No doubt,
Of all the other eminences passed,
'Tis justly named the veteran and chief !
Yosemite hotel is gained at last ;
Its Boniface receives ;—all find relief,—
His shrewd intelligence inspires one with belief.

XI.

Many a vale is beautiful like this ;
Not many though can boast of hills so steep,
Which mount so high, the sky above to kiss,
Aerial spirits there their vigils keep.
Its waterfalls are grand, but not so vast
As great Niagara. The " Mirror-lake,"
When not disturbed by zephyrs flitting past,
Reflects the mountain-sides, which re-awake
Echoes, repeated oft, when shots the silence break.

XII.

Imagination from the mountain heights,
From Glacier-point, and from the Sentinel,
    May inspiration draw,—take Fancy's flights,
Down the deep vale where fairies love to dwell;—
    Commune with angels on the heaped up piles
Of the Sierra; raised by Pluto's force
    Into huge billows for a thousand miles;
Yet rarely trod by foot of man or horse,
Its wealth will yield ere long unto the miner's course.

XIII.

The Architect Divine that planned the earth,
And charged the rocks with stores of wealth untold
    Foresaw that mankind from its earliest birth,
Would be attracted by the thirst of gold.
    Spain, Portugal, the Cassiterides
Drew ancient miners to their hills and plains.
    Chili, Peru, then Mexico, one sees
Coaxing Adventure for the miner's gains;
Despite its many sorrows, dangers, toil, and pains.

XIV.

Columbia approved, and straightway drew
To the three backbones which divide her states,
   An enterprising, reckless, daring crew
To probe the bowels of her rocks. The Fates
   Fickle success conferred, in no wise sure ;
Trade, Art, and Science followed in the wake—
   Heaven its work achieved.—Agriculture
Now claimed dominion. So, the plough and rake
Brought forth the real wealth Columbia bade them take.

XV.

Thus have the wonders of Columbia's land,
By mining enterprise been brought to light ;
   The vale Yosemite ! Its cliffs so grand !
Its trees enormous, of such wondrous height !
   Flora is charged with partiality,
In giving to the Californian state
   Coniferæ of such vitality,—
Growing for centuries ; so to create
Arborial monarchs—giants in height and weight.

XVI.

Where, in the world beside, can trees be found
Of feet exceeding three hundred in height ;
　With mammoth-stems one hundred feet around,
Whose branches thick, so high, fatigue the sight ?
　The " Grisly Giant " stands, tho' minus bark ;
The " fallen Monarch " now for worms is food ;
　And in this mammoth grove, one tree of mark
Still stands erect but rotten, black and rude,　[stood.
Wherein seven men on horse with perfect ease have

—•◦•—

THE GEYSERS.

I.

STURDY old Vulcan plies his trade,
  As well in East as West;
What kind of thunderbolts he made,
  Jove and the gods know best.
But in the realms Columbia rules,
  Many a forge's blast,
Where Cyclops wield huge ponderous tools,
  Roars out its thunder fast.

II.

Ofttimes a mountain range is found,
   With pangs of labour groaning;
Rolling in agony the ground,
   Trembling, sighing, moaning.
Many a chimney deep in earth,
   Down to internal fire,
Relieves its throes, by giving birth
   To flames which quick expire.

III.

Saline admixtures born are here,
   By Nature's alchemy;
" Gulches "* of California—
   Sweating up alkali.
Pluto resides somewhere about
   The Calistoga springs,
And from his lungs spurts sulphur out:
   Their praise, Fame loudly sings.

* Narrow valleys.

IV.

Famed are its baths for making limbs
   Flexible and lissom;
Improving skin—correcting whims,
   Expelling rheumatism,
The invalided—cured, return,
   Acting as advertisers;
The sickly—ever anxious yearn,
   For still more famous Geysers.

V.

The road thereto—some thirty miles—
   Winds round the mountains high—
Ledge (eight feet wide !) o'er steep defiles,
   The coach and four to try.
The driver, " Joss "—a " devil-dare,"
   Is in a state of bliss;
Down hill ! full gallop ! flying near
   The edge of precipice !

VI.

The slightest ! very slightest hitch !
　　Of horse—coach—Joss's dash,
This precious stage, and all—would pitch
　　To everlasting smash !
But naught goes wrong; the horses seem
　　To think this flying—fun ;
As downward rushes bounding-team,
　　At each successive run.

VII.

The *Canyons** high, the Gulches low,
　　Hills, crags, and waterfalls ;
The rippling river's plaintive flow—
　　Respond to Geysers' calls.
With alum-salts the ground is white :
　　The natives love to drink
Hot sulphur-water—their delight !
　　The same with "Devils' ink !"

* Mountain passes.

VIII.

This inkish-imp—in bottles sold,
　　When quiet, down doth settle.
But with a shake it springs up bold,
　　And shows his iron-mettle.
On paper white, if writ it stains ;
　　'Tis found in " Devil's-holes :"
He uses it whene'er he gains
　　By contract—human souls !

IX.

At Devil's Cauldron—witches' haunt !
　　They mix in steam their spells ;
And from the " Devil's pulpit " chaunt
　　The marvels of the Fells.
Here Nature's baths from earth upsteam,
　　Of sulphur, salt, or iron ;
Poets therein of future dream,
　　And laurel wreaths rely on.

x.

Vegetation here is rich indeed !
　　Despite of alkali ;
The finny-tribes likewise can breed,
　　In river rolling by.
The Geysers in wild loveliness—
　　Romantic, gorgeous, fair !
Provoke reflection—God to bless,
　　For all such blessings rare !

MORMONS.

I.

Almighty God ! by Thy divine command
Moses his hosts, o'er desert and o'er sea,
For forty years, led to the Holy Land—
The promised land ! and promised too by Thee.
This long-wished goal, when first brought into sight,
Did westward lie, beyond the Jordan vale,—
Then held by Moabite and Canaanite,
Where soaring mountains still confirm the tale.

II.

We've climbed these mounts, albeit with many a halt;
The waves have breasted in the salt Dead Sea;
Bathed in the Jordan, to wash off its salt,
And seen its now degraded misery.
Here dwelt Thy chosen people, until sin
Coax'd them from Virtue's paths and Thy high will.
Slavery her portals opened,—they went in;
Oft did they wander,—they are wanderers still.

III.

Time turned his sand-glass and the earth toiled on;
Thou in Thy mercy sent Thy Son divine,
Who in this Jordan was baptized by John:
His birth so low made more His glory shine.
His followers too were all of humble birth,
That left their nets, the crook, the flail, and plough,
To teach Christ's law, that peace might dwell on earth,
Goodwill to man—to God, in reverence bow.

IV.

Since our thrice bless'd Redeemer's crucifixion
Full eighteen centuries have passed away
In the far west, and, using English diction,
A sect exists,—"Saints of the latter day."
Like every sect that boasts of Lord and cross,
They claim a mission quite direct from God:
They've suffered pillage, persecution, loss,
But live and thrive under affliction's rod.

V.

Between the Mormon and the Jewish land
A certain parallel well traced may be:
Each has a large sweet-water lake at hand;
A river Jordan, and a Dead salt-sea.
That in the West is named the Utah Lake,
While in the East 'tis Lake of Galilee:
A Jordan river from each one doth make
A channel deep, to set its water free.

VI.

In Mormon State, Lake Utah's raised aloft
Four thousand feet *above* Pacific main!
From south, through Jordan, rolls its burthen soft
Into Salt Lake, at north end of the plain.
But in the sacred vale of Palestine,
From Galilee, southward is Jordan's flow;
Bearing its flood into the Dead Sea brine,
More than a *thousand* feet depressed *below!*

VII.

Each Jordan vale in width is much the same;
So with the mountains which command each vale.
To Moab's heights the Jews with Moses came,
Despite all perils at which mortals quail.
The Wahsatch range is Utah's eastern wall,
Where Brigham's van arrived in '47:
He gazed below—like Moses, vowed his call
Was to yon wilderness, by will of Heaven.

VIII.

Suspicion whispered—then came unbelief,
That such a "howling wilderness" could yield
Aught else than disappointment, toil, and grief;
Till the Saints' leader, looking far a-field,
Declared that God would bless them with His aid,
Would send them water, rain, or mist, or dew,
If with devoted hearts they reverence paid,
And joined but willing hands to hearts as true.

IX.

After due search "canyons" * were found, wherein
Springs were discovered bubbling from the hills;
Conduits upsprang—the water flowed therein,
Descending from the mains in plenteous rills.
Each tract of land, when settled in the plain,
Was thus supplied to irrigate the sand :
And soon each farmer found that toil meant gain,
When bounteous crops of cereals blessed his land.

* Ravines, or passes, in American mountains.

X.

The surplus water which the soil could spare,
Flowed in clear channels both sides of each street;
Pomona blessed their work—fruits rich and rare,
In Utah's gardens everywhere you meet.
In Salt Lake city locust-trees are found,
Edging the footway—so the path to shade:
They flourish bravely—rootlets through the ground
Imbibing moisture from the channels made.

XI.

The vale here viewed from top of Ensign-peak—
(A prom'nent rock)—the Mormons this allege,—
The signal was, which Brigham had to seek
As resting place—so the Almighty pledge.
After a thousand miles of prairie, rock,
Vast rivers, Indians, and of toils severe;
Pursued by murder, pillage, and the shock
Of storm and want, the Mormons settled here.

XII.

The city viewed from here—lies at your feet,
Like sparkling brilliants set in emeralds rare ;
An Eden garden, breathing odours sweet:
Damascus-like—smaller—but quite as fair.
The winding Jordan is a silver thread,
Peeping thro' trees, far as the eye can reach ;
Bearing fresh tribute to the Salt Lake—dead—
Stretched out between a hundred miles of beach.

XIII.

Such is this valley now—but 'twas not so
Two decades since, when Indian-hunting ground :
Then weeds-saline and scrubby grass would grow :
Wild men, and animals, and snakes were found.
But Enterprise and Industry combined,
And soon in place of weeds a garden grew ;
The farmer's toil, quick recompense did find ;
And earth, now fruitful, yielded crops anew.

XIV.

Then homesteads quickly rose, surrounded by
Fences of wood, or "adobe," (sun-dried brick :)
A Thespian temple ; and still soaring high—
Their Tabernacle, o'er the foliage thick.
Oval in form—so high, for miles is seen ;
Colossal in its width as well as length :
Without a single column intertween :
Its roof sustained by wall-piers great in strength.

XV.

Its vast interior, fifteen thousand souls
Accommodates.   This decent, pious host
Rises *en masse*, as the grand organ rolls,
Praise to the Father, Son, and Holy Ghost !
For all the sin that's past,—a fervent prayer
Pleads for condonement.   The sexes sit apart,—
Skilled music fills the space, and many a tear
Follows a sermon touching head and heart.

XVI.

The difference is but slight, 'tween Salt Lake town,
And other cities of Columbia's states :
From Great Pacific rail is carried down
The iron way, which runs at Mormon-rates,—
As free to enter as it is to quit.
Here divers trades, and folk, and sects abound ;
Gaming and dram-shops, Yankees up have set,
Against the Mormon-grain, on Mormon ground.

XVII.

The Mormon mind is simple, bold, and frank,
Honest, truthful, sober—and cheerful too ;
In all good men's esteem, they high would rank,
If Polygamic charges were not true.
'Tis true too often 'mongst Monogamists,
Pairs ill-assorted pass to grief and strife—
(Adulterous sinners,) till Divorce insists
On bursting bonds that held them man and wife.

M

XVIII.

Of Mormon origin (they this allege)
A very poor, but serious, pious boy,
Received, in answer to his prayer, a pledge
From the Lord's angel, that he should employ
His future life in founding a new sect.
Joe Smith—this boy was named—in faith so firm !
His friends and kindred marvell'd.   They elect
Him chief and priest, till end of his life's term.

XIX.

It is alleged that Smith, in '23,
Sought out " Cumorah " Hill, near to the town
Of Manchester, in New York state ; that he
Met with this hill—therein, well covered down,
A book he found, of plates " alike to gold :"
Each side of plate had characters well graved—
Egyptian glyphics small.—These, to unfold,
His way with light from Heaven then was paved.

XX.

So Mormon's book relates what " Ether "* wrote,

Six hundred years before our Saviour's time ;

How, when the Lord proud Babel-tower smote,

Some of the scattered reached the Western clime.

That their descendants spread o'er Western world,

Building them temples, then Chaldean styled :

How Satan followed, and how soon them hurled

To idol-worship and to Indians wild.

XXI.

Well, 'tis alleged in Mormon's book, that this

Old history of fifteen hundred years,

By Ether writ with priestly emphasis—

Fell to the Israelites, who, it appears,

Of Joseph's seed, fled to the far, far west.

This seed took root, and thence two tribes upsprang—

" Nephi " and " Laman "—soon these tribes did test,

The ancient Jewish feuds, with hostile clang.

* A Jewish priest, who escaped with some of his tribe at the time of the first Babylonish captivity ; and succeeded in reaching the Western hemisphere. Mormon, who wrote A. D. 400, affirms that this Ether collected the traditions of the Chaldeans, who first reached America; and compiled their history during a period of 1500 years.

XXII.

It is affirmed, by aid of this same light,—
With scribes appointed, some to testify,—
By time, toil, patience, Smith's prophetic sight
Deciphered what all else did mystify.
So the translation swelled beneath his hands;
It was unfolded how a certain priest,
Mormon by name, obeying God's commands,
Traced how his tribes migrated from the East :—

XXIII.

How, after Christ four hundred years had passed,
He lived and wrote—abridging books before—
Foreseeing that his nation would not last:
His son, Maroni, added to it more.
Then, by the will divine, the book was laid
Most carefully in hill of Cumorah;
There to lie hidden, till God's will be made
Known to the Jews—" Deliverance is not far."

XXIV.

The tribe of Nephi was a godly race;
A thousand years this nation's life could boast:
Their priests were worthy, could the future trace,
Preached of the Saviour, felt the Holy Ghost!
There, in the Western world, as in the East,
God's chosen people could not keep from sin:
Envy and Malice gave Satanic feast;
Asked were the tribes—they came with all their kin.

XXV.

The vengeance of the Lord flies near and far!
Cities destroyed, the tribes now ceased from toil,
But seized on hunting-grounds, made fiendish war,
And Satan pleased by devilish deeds of spoil.
This Mormon, like Josephus, could foresee
The ruin of his race on western soil,
And therefore gave abridged their pedigree,
And how they were involved in ruin's coil.

XXVI.

Mormon, a Jew from Joseph's seed derived—
So it is said—having this book compiled,
Passed to his fathers.　But his son contrived—
(Maroni, of the Nephi priesthood, styled)—
To add thereto full twenty years of lore,
About the Church and all its sacred rites,
A thousand years upon Columbia's shore,—
Then hid the book from treacherous Lamanites.

XXVII.

For fourteen centuries in hill concealed—
The Indian races wild, a mystery still—
The hiding-place was to Joe Smith revealed.
After four years, to him came light and skill
To solve the problem of the Indian red;
To found the "Church of God," to clear the way
For restitution of all Jews, who're led
To join his Church—"Saints of the Latter Day."

XXVIII.

This Church affirms, no priest of God can be
Unless so called by revelations clear :
That worldly wisdom fails to make eyes see
The Lord's commands, which to the saints appear.
By inspiration clearly, well defined,
They claim to heal the sick, by touch, by prayer;
To learn the will of the Almighty mind,
And shape their course thereby, from year to year.

XXIX.

While other sects assert their strong *belief,*
They, from internal promptings, say—they *know.*
They send their missions forth, at notice brief,
Without due funds; trusting the Lord will show
How food and raiment for the morrow come.
Having made proselytes, in three years' time
Return with " crown of grace " to Mormon-home—
Founding " God's Church " in every distant clime.

XXX.

Thus they affirm arose the Mormon creed—
So humbly born : Jesus was lowly too !
Most of whose followers were men of need,
Daring the hate of heathen as of Jew.
Most of the pilgrims first, across the main,
Fled from religious persecution of the East :
Their children hate in like unchristian vein,
And treat the polygamic Mormon as a beast.

XXXI.

Is it the devil's work, or is 't God's will
That every sect should own some cause of strife ?
The sacred prophecies He will fulfil,
When He sees fit—restoring temporal life
Unto the seed of Joseph.   Utah State
Owns Priests (Melchisedek as well as Aaron),
Elders, Apostles—and the prophets wait
The Jews to welcome *there*, instead of *Sharon*.

———◦◦◦———

THE LOWER MISSISSIPPI.

I.

The Mississippi, of all floods the chief,
Like the grand monarch of a Sylvan grove,
  By its main trunk affords well-timed relief
To branches vast, feeding where e'er they rove.
  This trunk in Mexican Gulf fixes its roots,
Receiving all the mighty waterflow,
  Which forms the greater twigs and lesser shoots
Of giant branches. Branches which swell and grow
To trunk-like size, e'er trunk gains Gulf of Mexico.

II.

And then what mighty rivers are they all
That form the Western branches of the trunk—
    Rolling thro' kingdom-states, to where they fall
Into main-stem—the streams which they have drunk.
    So the Red-river—Indiana drains;
Helped by Arkansas, which too Kansas serves.
    The turbid Missouri Dacotah gains,
As well Nebraska, thro' whose vales it swerves;
And high Dacotah's lands and Montana's preserves.

III.

So, with the eastern branches of this tree—
The Ohio, that drains Ohio state,
    Virginia, Kentuck, and State Tennessee—
The Illinois, tho' large is not so great,
    But drains the Illinoisan-prairies well.
So the Wisconsin and St. Croix combined,
    Serve Michigan, where many miners dwell.
'Midst all these branches emigrants can find,
Mount, mine, vale, river-work, of every varied kind.

IV.

Below the spot where great Missouri flows
Into the Mississippi-trunk, there stands
   The famed St. Louis ! whose dominion grows
Greater each year, that commerce lends its hands
   To pile up its magnificence.   For here,
Five decades since—no more ! was the " far-west,"
   Now moved two thousand miles beyond, to where
The great Pacific rolls its ocean crest
Upon the western coasts, which here the States invest.

V.

In fair St. Louis, French and blacks abound;
The town is fine—a thousand miles from sea !
   'Tis mostly built on elevated ground :
It boasts no docks, but an extensive quay,
   A depot for the north as well as west;
Whose mighty offerings its proud flood doth bear,
   State-house, hotels, theatres of the best,
Much wealth, good schools, an annual state-fair :
Commerce and Enterprise are well rewarded here !

VI.

This famous fair affords a wide spread lap,
Flora, Pomona, Ceres, therein fling
   Productions rich and vast.   All this to cap,
Apollo and skilled Mercury both bring
   Rare treasures coined by Science and by Art !
Its circus is the largest in the west
   Where trotting horses take an active part :
Shows, mountebanks and minstrels do their best [guest.
To charm the Yankee mind, and please the stranger-

VII.

When fairs prevail, the town is overfull ;
Hotels are crammed—each chamber filled with beds,
   And travellers mix, that don't together pull.
He quick departs who such discomfort dreads,
   And gains a berth on board a river-boat.
Many are moored all-times the quay beside—
   A change agreeable to hotel afloat !
A thousand miles therein you choose to ride,
Regardless of all risks—if good, if ill betide.

VIII.

On the deck (hurricane,) we paced at night;
The bustling town ablaze with gas-light glare !

Unveiled the sky,—for gods a glorious sight !
How beautiful ! how marvellous ! how rare !

The moon is at the full—her flood of light
Outshines the stars, at other times so fair !

E'en brilliant Venus now shows far less bright.
How still is Nature ! scarce a breath of air :
But man's astir on flood, with anxious thought and care.

IX.

The placid flood, grateful for Cynthia's beams,
Reflects her face, the sky, the boats, the trees,

As deep below, as sky above, it seems!
How gratitude begets the wish to please !

Sometimes a river punt would cross the stream,
Too far beneath the fall of oar to hear.

Majestic steamers would to Fancy's dream,
Colossal swans with twin black necks appear,
Their monster bodies white, flapping huge wings as fair.

x.

So light such craft, it seems of pasteboard made;
And yet, when close, so tight, so tough, so swift!
With glaring lamps from every part betrayed!
Its mighty wings, when flapping, fairly lift
The monster body from its aqueous nest.
Nearer it comes, and vomits blackened fume:
Then utters shrieks—its well-known signal test:
Now sturdy blacks uncover package dome,
Throw stage and hawsers out, and clear for passage-room.

xi.

These river boats are mostly dressed in white,
With gilding, mirrors, and rich woods inlaid:
One straight saloon (three hundred feet),—the height
To correspond. The berths—two each—are made
In cabins on both sides of the saloon.
The outer doors all open on the guard,
Running the boat all round; so that you soon
Attain this spacious and long promenade.
The barber cuts and shaves, is fiddler, and is bard.

XII.

Near all large towns villas oft rise to view
Upon the river-banks.   Stations are met
   At frequent intervals, as boat steams through
The yielding flood, with many shoals beset;
   High bluffs and green-topp'd hills on either side.
If banks be low, high *levees* there are made.
   Four hundred miles of run, the boat doth ride
In mouth of Ohio, for Cairo's trade,—
The famous Eden Swamp Mark Tapley did parade!

XIII.

When this vast flood is at its utmost height,
Some *levees* burst, and banks are worn away ;
   Extensive lakes are formed, so pilots' sight
Must learn these channels where the waters stray.
   He tingles bell, to test by plumb and line
Where shallows lurk; then comes the lead-man's strain,
   As through his hands speeds quick the knotted twine,
" A quarter past,"—" A quarter to Mark-twain,"*
Till sure of depth again—the lead is thrown again.

* Twain is two fathoms.

XIV.

And in an instant, with another bell,
He signals to the engineer below ;
  Without a word this officer can tell,
"To right or left," "to ease," "go fast or slow."
  In "pilot-house," high up some forty feet,
The watchful, well-trained pilot turns the wheel ;
  . With eagle's eye he scans the liquid sheet,
And through its windings guides the shallow keel :
Should this scrape river-bed, a tremor quick you feel.

XV.

On the east side of Mississippi's flood
Stands Memphis city—Memphis of the West !
  More than three thousand years ago there stood
An ancient Memphis, then amongst the best
  Of Egypt's cities on west bank of Nile !
Where are thy glories now, O Memphis old ?
  Thy monarchs proud ? thy palaces ? thy style ?
From Cheops' top the sight can still unfold
Thy ruins grand, o'er which the desert sands have rolled !

XVI.

Then proud Sesostris, in his regal might,
Compelled the negro-slaves his will obey.
  Now in this Western Memphis, freedom's right
Has dashed the fetters from their limbs away.
  Here, now, as then, upon Nile's bank, the sun
Seeks the horizon with effulgence rare;
  The sky is all aglow—day's race is run—
The liquid mirror claims her glory's share:
And heaven's roseate tints deep in the flood appear!

XVII.

Memphis is high, so down her shelving banks,
Large bales of cotton quick are rolled along;
  At every station, now these bales—in ranks,
Bound up in canvas, with hoop-iron strong,
  Await the river boats to New Orleans.
Four thousand such they somehow stow away!
  Think for a moment, what such burden means!
Besides all other freight, how long they stay!
The cost of such a load! how well these packets pay!

N

XVIII.

When boats are crowded quite to overflow,
Two, three, more barges are made fast to side :
The freight in them doth still more mighty grow,
As down the flood the stately bark doth glide.
The mates are Yankees, whose quick, sharp commands
Keep crew of blacks alert at such slave-work :
All freight is promptly moved beneath their hands :
At intervals they rest—but dare not shirk
The orders stern of mate, or captain, or the clerk.

XIX.

At Vicksburg, Natchez, and a host beside,
Of towns and stations on this wealthy flood,
The monster boat, its round prow turns to side
Of landing place, and thrusts broad plank of wood
To join, as bridge, the boat unto the shore.
Both passengers and freight are quickly changed ;
The captain lifts his hand—the steam-throats roar—
Bridge quick withdrawn, and all new freight arranged,
Bells ring from pilot-house—" she's off "—nought is
[deranged.

xx.

Life on the Mississipp'—in truth 'tis strange !
Three thousand miles in length—one single flood ;
  Above, high verdant lands—a constant change,
Here rugged bluffs, and there primeval wood.
  The boats side-wheeled, or screw, or wheel astern ;
Huge timber rafts, and snags, now and again :
  When flood is low, each pilot has to learn
The treacherous shoals, which oft the boat detain :
Sometimes the sky will glow from fires upon the plain.

PRAIRIE FIRES.

I.

THE rolling prairie, and the swamp dried up,
   Are easily incited to inflame ;
Then fiery serpents on the parched sward sup.
   Like hydra-headed snakes, they scorch and maim
All within reach.   Each darts his lambent tongue
   From head upraised, on high and twisted neck.
The searing venom from its fang is wrung—
   Hissing and spitting, with but little check,—
The poisoned breath bequeaths one black and smould-
                   ['ring wreck.

II.

And if the ironway on joists be laid,
   These withering serpents as they crawl along,
Devour sleepers and their bed so made—
   The irons fall, and then the train goes wrong.
Their human freight and packages as well,
   O'er the black crackling embers have to pass,
Mosquito-legions leave their marks to tell.—
   Brigades of hopping insects, from the grass,
Chirrup a lively chorus, to sustain the farce.

III.

The hours chase each other while you wait;
   Anxiety doth reign in every face;
The sun retires from his throne of state :
   Celestial orbs—the threatening clouds efface.
Mosquitos' buzz you hear, their sting you feel,
   On face not veiled, or covered o'er with hair;
The hands in gloves also,—gloves are not steel—
   Blood sucking insects can no pity share,
You're pitted in the morn, so that a saint would swear.

IV.

Perched upon trunks and bags, creation's lords
    Look black and growl, and hands and kerchiefs shake,
They blow a cloud, which little ease affords;
    From rich blood veins, their thirst the stingers slake,
The hopping-insects chirp a serenade;
    Faces are slapped—"a playing on the bones;"
Determined sufferers on them make a raid,
    Numbers are smashed. You fail to hear their moans,
You hear the thud, as well the smashers' angry groans.

V.

Is "Patience" virtue? you perforce must wait;
    Columbia's rails have but a single track
When quiet convenient, at a moderate rate,
    The train approaches, and its speed they slack.
And now a rush is made the cars to gain;
    Beware of falling!—'tis a broken limb,
Your friends the "suckers" politely refrain
    From entering first, but being quick and slim,
They buzz around your head their tiny wings of film.

VI.

Where e'er the flames have licked, the rolling grass
  Has changed to fire—left a charred ash.
The feathered tribe affrighted from it pass,
  The startled buffaloes their haunches lash
With furious tail impelled by fear and dread,
  Their roar like thunder sounds, the earth they shake,
As from the flames they bound, each bristling head
  Straining to leeward, as full speed they make,
To 'scape the blazing foe—seek rivulet or lake.

VII.

The lesser fauna, with but feeble power
  Such peril to avoid, are caught and killed.
The vulture, hawk and eagle o'er them lower :
  The air with moaning and tumult is filled.
And graceful antelope, like maiden fair,
  Starts with a scream, and looks for company ;
And at her utmost speed, bounds off to where
  Its frightened mates uncertain, restlessly
Await the strongest hind to teach the way to flee.

VIII.

The fiery serpent-host advances on
    As an invading army o'er the land;
Maintaining strength by what it feeds upon :
    But failing that, it fails to hold command.
The prairie grasses, flowers, and the sage,
    Are speedily consumed—scorched are the trees.
The white man checks its ardent, hissing rage,
    By mowing belt of meadow—so he frees,
His homestead from the foe, which he surveys at ease.

———•———

THE "ITALY."

I.

CLOSE alongside a Hudson-river wharf,
Lies the huge steamer, "Italy" by name ;
  Each passing tug compared is but a dwarf;
To Liverpool she's bound, and thence she came,
  Four thousand tons she swallows for her freight ;
The upper deck four hundred feet is long :
  To the "Great Eastern" she is next the great !
Iron—her body ; so, to keep it strong,
Are masts and spars also that nothing may go wrong.

II.

This splendid ship now lets her hawsers go,
Apollo, pleased, looks on with all his smiles;
   Serene the air, propitious zephyrs blow;
Staten, the Governor's, and other isles
   Flit quickly by; Long Island claims a look.
Now out at sea, the pilot quits the bark—
   Up go the sails.   We now pass Sandy-hook.
The captain, Grace, four officers of mark   [dark.
Bravely the vessel guide through daylight and through

III.

So large a ship a numerous crew requires;
Many they are, and each is at his post;
   Skilled engineers, and those who charge the fires,
Vie with each other to excel the most.
   Their doctor, Digges, is courteous and kind;
The cook is able, all the meals well served;
   Cabins are large.   The berths are clean we find.
A few are sick at first, but soon get nerved: [swerved.
Eastward the vessel's course, from which she rarely

IV.

Oft in his berth at night—lamps being out,
Supine one lies, as though in coffin stretched;
  For window, just a port-hole kind of spout;
With footfalls over head, when crew is fetched.
  Up the horizon the dim twilight creeps,
And through the dancing port is faintly shown.
  The coffined tourist fancies 'twixt his sleeps,
The shaft, that turns the screw, grinds forth a moan;
" We are going alone ! we are going alone !"

V.

Hark ! 'tis eight bells, and time the watch be changed;
The winds grow fierce and sweep from stern to prow:
  On main and foremast, many sails are ranged,
Which, pregnant by the winds, do labour now.
  The evening star dances between the sheets—
A lamp in truth placed in the firmament !
  The monster vessel, every wave it meets,
Dashes to atoms ; which as spray is sent
To after part of ship,—here is its fury spent.

VI.

Bright Cynthia now is half way up the sky,
And sheds a flood of light upon the deep;
 The deep!—that's true—'tis rising mountains high!
'Tis difficult one's pace on deck to keep.
 Each valley 'twixt the crested mountain waves
Seems gulf enough to swallow up the ship;
 But she—so brave, so tight, so well behaves!
Just mounts upon the crest, and then doth dip,
Like to a graceful swan, that curves its neck to sip.

VII.

Huge snowy, alpine clouds margin the sea;
And truant mists are flitting overhead;
 Not all the stars to-night on watch will be:
The Milky Way is not;—it may have fed
 The Little Dog, the Great and Lesser Bear.
The Pleiades are winking at the theft,
 Because, forsooth the Lady in the Chair
Has fallen asleep; tho' she in charge is left
Of the Lacteal Zone, of which she's now bereft.

VIII.

Zephyrs are fickle ! November found them so ;
And so they got the port side of the prow :
　Then willing sails grew pregnant with their blow ;
But when they charged due east, the sheets were now
　Hauled down.　Vapours into huge masses crowd—
Shedding erratic tears, as for a friend—
　And drape the vault of heaven with a shroud.
Apollo sometimes would his glories send :
Thus did it alternate until our journey's end.

IX.

Aurora's slumbers are prolonged each morn ;
But Vesper, earlier from his couch doth rise :
　The waning year month ofter month is shorn,
And Phœbus mounts still lower in the skies.
　Just as the winds were on their message sent,
So did their breath feel hot, or cold, or wet ;
　If at the prow they bounced, we stayed ; but went
Dashing along, if either shipside met
The gusty offspring which Æolus can beget.

x.

Oft, leaden skies shut out Celestial hosts ;
The gallant ship being tossed from fore to aft ;
From Neptune's deep, the drowned departed ghosts
Helped the wind's chorus, as they grimly laughed :
They clutched the bulwarks ; came not on the deck.
The rolling waves, piled up in many a dome,
Joined in the chorus, 'bout some fearful wreck !
The screw propelled against the sparkling foam, [home."
Shrieks out—"We are going home, we are going

xi.

All things have endings ; so, thank God, have storms :
The sea went down, tho' sails were strained and tight ;
The blue green deep frothed foam of varied forms,
Like undulating waves of Malachite.
O'er head, were massing still vast Cumuli :
One heap obscured the rising orb of day,
Whose light so fell on lower clouds hard by—
Them scooped in gorges deep,—each separate ray
Silvering their alpine tops, as seen on mountain way.

XII.

The Decalogue ordains each seventh day,
Should be a day of rest to honour Him,
  Who made the heavens, earth, and Milky Way.
So everything on deck is taut and trim,
  For Sunday-morning service.   Very well
The surgeon of the ship performed this work :
  Psalm and prayer books were opened at "sixth bell."
Cards, chess, and draughts, each one was fain to shirk,
Each grateful passenger acting as "Amen" clerk.

XIII.

At length, Queenstown is reached, and some depart ;
Pilot on board—the ship now speeds along :
  On the "port quarter," come the winds so smart,
Its sheets swell out, under such pressure strong. [drunk
  Champagne goes round, good-luck and health are
To company, to officers, and crew.
  Well have they acted, nor from hardships shrunk.
The Mersey gained, and Liverpool in view,
  Then search at Custom-house for claims to custom due.

———◦◦◦———

FAREWELL, COLUMBIA!

I.

FAREWELL, Columbia ! Fate may not permit
Once more the pleasure to revisit thee :
    Bright glows the lamp Experience has lit
For those who cross the deep Atlantic sea.
    Thy harbours, rivers, boats, thy railway cars,
Falls, mountains, dells, one profits much to see :
    Thy flags, which flaunt with brilliant stripes and stars,
Thy noble schools, for education free ;
Thy customs, manners, faults, whatever they may be.

II.

Each nation has its faults, and thou hast thine,
—Thine, (criticised without the just excuse,)
   Bid fast thy liberty to undermine,
By licence getting loose. Why then refuse,
   As palliative, that, on thy friendly shore,
The floods of emigrants do oft descend,—
   Welcomed by freedom, scarcely known before,
At first these oft with vulgar pride offend;
Their offspring, being schooled, will to good order bend.

III.

Then with the fiery Celt, and stolid Frank;
The scum of Europe comes, thief, runaway,—
   And with the worthy mix. Such cannot rank
'Mongst citizens of merit—albeit they stay,
   And play the ruffians on Columbia's stage;
Evading skilfully the baffled laws,
   'Till hanged, or shot by Lynch, in his just rage.
The scales by Justice held, have holes and flaws, [cause.
All strangers note this well. Such scum is here one

IV.

The Southern states, up to a recent date,
In slavery held all the Negro race :
  Nor in the north was changed their bonded state,
Till Europe urged Columbia to efface
  The slave-stain, from her flag so striped and starred.
Columbia knew 'twas hostile to the creed
  Of Christian sects ; moreover, that it barred
Her claim for asking Justice to concede
Her sons, that high esteem, for which most nations greed.

V.

Columbia, by her influence with force,
Has freed the bondsman throughout all her realms :
  This change, the south accepts without remorse,
Freedom first dazzles, and then overwhelms,
  Those whom she liberates, with duties new.
With other labour free they now compete :
  Many industrious are, but not a few
Disrelish freedom, since they have to meet
Necessities with which free laws all freemen greet.

VI.

Millions of blacks, now having citizen's rights,
Struggle for work, wealth, place and power too ;
   Sometimes they are insolent—have reckless fights,
Creating civic complications new.
   Thousands of coolies from celestial clime,
Compete with negroes, Irish, and Franks :
   Columbia anxiously prospects the time, .
When education shall elicit thanks
From all this motley mass, when joined to order's ranks.

VII.

Columbia by her majesty and will, .
Has placed the sceptre in Republic's hands.
   Vast is its sway indeed ! and vaster still
Its sway will grow, as o'er such mighty lands
   The tide of emigration onward flows.
Her difficulties most enormous are !
   Columbia's genius—as Republic grows—
Will grasp them all—so render popular
The sway, 'neath which flaunts flag with stripe and star.

VIII.

Under Columbia's protecting care,
The march of education will be blessed,
　High morality with common sense will pair,
And charity beget—by all caressed.
　Columbia sees that her Democracy,
Demands both moral worth and intellect,
　To cope with statesmen in diplomacy.
Peace to maintain at home—from war protect—
Justice and law maintain—licence of sin correct !

www.ingramcontent.com/pod-product-compliance
Lightning Source LLC
Chambersburg PA
CBHW030539040726
47497CB00008B/2521